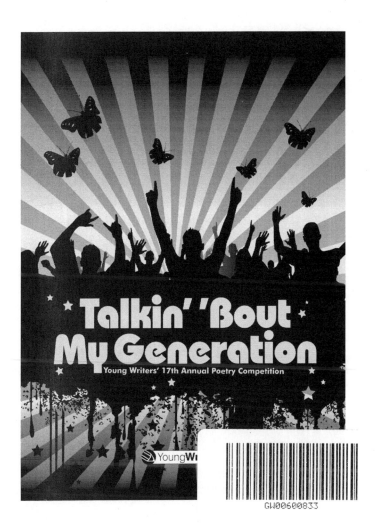

Talkin' 'Bout My Generation

Young Writers' 17th Annual Poetry Competition

YoungW...

GW00600833

Essex

Edited by Angela Fairbrace

 Young**Writers**

First published in Great Britain in 2008 by:
Young Writers
Remus House
Coltsfoot Drive
Peterborough
PE2 9JX
Telephone: 01733 890066
Website: www.youngwriters.co.uk

© *Copyright Contributors 2007*

SB ISBN 978-1 84431 433 1

Foreword

This year, the Young Writers' *Talkin' 'Bout My Generation* competition proudly presents a showcase of the best poetic talent selected from thousands of up-and-coming writers nationwide.

Young Writers was established in 1991 to promote the reading and writing of poetry within schools and to the young of today. Our books nurture and inspire confidence in the ability of young writers and provide a snapshot of poems written in schools and at home by budding poets of the future.

The thought, effort, imagination and hard work put into each poem impressed us all and the task of selecting poems was a difficult but nevertheless enjoyable experience.

We hope you are as pleased as we are with the final selection and that you and your family continue to be entertained with *Talkin' 'Bout My Generation Essex* for many years to come.

Contents

Chalvedon School & Sixth Form College

Ceri Hopkinson (13)	23
Rebecca Taylor (14)	23
Conor Herbing (13)	24
Charlotte Cornwall (15)	24
Chloe McCarthy (13)	25
Robert Duckworth-Coyne (13)	25

Emerson Park School

Harry Smith (12)	26
Alice Green (13)	26
Kemal Cetinay (11)	27
Lewis Shacklady (12)	27
Jack Quinlan (11)	28
Molly Jones (11)	28
Lee Robertson (12)	29
Paul Constable (12)	29
Richard Manton (11)	30
Charlotte Brinsmead (12)	30
Grace Levy (11)	31
Abigail Dowling (13)	31
Billy Fitzpatrick (14)	32
Elizabeth Chapman (13)	33
Kate Norris (12)	34
Jonathan McFarlane (13)	34
Aimée Sell (12)	35
George Estcourt(13)	36
Bethany Wells (13)	36
Tyler Gibbs (12)	37
Toni Murley (12)	37
Harry Culham (13)	38
Jordan Braidwood (12)	39
Connor Squibb (11)	40
Filza Mahmood (13)	40
Ellie Constantine (11)	41
Matt Brett (12)	41
Laine Swaby (12)	42
Ronnie Scott (12)	43

Gaynes School

Charlie McGinley (13)	44
Alice White (12)	44

Hall Mead School

Helena Romanes School

Honywood Community Science School

John Matthews (12)	87
Emily Smith (11)	88
Jody Morris (12)	88
Lucy Pike (11)	89
Sam Smith	89
Charlotte Wilson (11)	90
Alec Willett (11)	91
Kerry Hasler (11)	91
Rebecca Franklin	92
Laura Newlove	92
Shannon Barrett (11)	93
Leigh-Anne Weller	93
Chloe Humphreys	94

The Sanders Draper School

Zack McGuinness (13)	94
Michael Buckland (13)	95
Mitchell Webb (13)	95
Elliot Barker (13)	96
George Goodey (13)	96
Rebecca Willats (14)	97
Chloe Smith (13)	97
Jack Turton (14)	98
Lauren Thomas (13)	98
Rosie Bailey (13)	99
Kaffy Ayofe (13)	99
Kirsty Mills (12)	100
Belmira Okoro (11)	100
Tom McGovern (14)	101
Danielle Thomas (13)	101
Ross Woolward (12)	102
Michael Wilson (12)	103
Sophie Furlong (12)	103
Maxine Nhin (12)	104
Jayne Hardy (12)	104
Lydia Butler (13)	105
Ashley Burdett (13)	105
Brooke Cooper (12)	106
Govinda Tiwari (12)	106
Samantha Harris (12)	107
Sophie Reynolds (12)	107

Josh Jervis (13)	129
Katie Watkins (14)	130
Michael Vann (13)	130
Aaron Baker (11)	131
Martin Winter	131
Monica Gurung (13)	132
Kerry Moorby (13)	132
Lauren Forsyth (13)	133
Emma Green (13)	133
Maddie Scates (11)	134
Beki Humm (14)	135
Jade Stockwell (13)	136
Lauren Annette (11)	137
Sophie Glasson (13)	138
Fay Oxby (11)	138
Liam Bond (12)	139
Ryan Tierney (13)	139
Alexandra Smith (14)	140
Callum Pearce (11)	140
Harry Hannigan (13)	141
Alexandra Roberts (11)	141
Emily Houillon (11)	142
Catherine Burling (13)	143
Emma Farrow (11)	144
Amy Howell (12)	144
Ellis Davis (11)	145
Hayley Waggon (13)	145
Lily Cook (11)	146
Ben Franklin (11)	146
Molly Humphreys (11)	147
James Prince (13)	147
Claudia Shaw (11)	148
Katie Rankin (11)	148
Ben Cox (13)	149
Jaymee Wilkinson (11)	149
Bradley Batt (11)	150
Jaime-Leigh Mason (11)	150
Matt Dunt	151
Dale Bliss (13)	151
Jaydon Kinnaird (13)	152
Charlie Jones (13)	152
Kathryn Bowen (11)	153

The Poems

My Generation

Generation, generation,
So many to be found,
Young, old, all ages,
My generation is now,
It's the generation for me.

iPods, mp3s, digital cameras,
All sorts of gizmos.
Mobiles to use,
Songs to download,
It's my generation.

Fun is here,
Life's like a roller coaster,
Fabulous fashion,
With beanpole models,
This is my generation.

Computers and game consoles,
Cinemas to go to,
Films to watch,
My generation is . . .
Simply the best.

New technology is everywhere,
Generations change,
Get bigger and better,
I wouldn't change
My generation,
For anything.

Becky Lowry (13)
Chalvedon School & Sixth Form College

My Generation

It all started with my mum and dad's mum and dad,
They had my mum and dad,
They had me and my four sisters.

It all started when I went to play school,
I met friends,,
They played with me, doing building.

It all started at nursery,
I met my old friends and made new friends,
I played and painted.

It all started at Whitmore Infant School,
I went with my old friends and I made new friends,
I worked my little hands off.

It all started at Whitmore Junior School,
I went with my old friends and I made new friends,
I worked my hands off, with a little bit of homework.

It all started at Chalvedon,
I went with my old friend and I made new friends,
I worked my big head off, with a lot of homework.

Katrina Frow (13)
Chalvedon School & Sixth Form College

All Me

All you hear in my generation is cars racing up and down
When they race there is a winner and he will be crowned
Football is my passion,
Armani and Nike are my fashion,
I'm a l'il kid with spiky hair
And I never can decide what to wear!
I like graffiti, it is cool,
Using spray on wall to wall.
Ssshhh!

Bill Holloway (12)
Chalvedon School & Sixth Form College

The Things We Take For Granted

The things we take for granted,
The things you never had,
The miles you walked to school,
The bus I always use,
What is this generation we live in,
The things we take for granted?

The world we live in today,
The wars you thought would stay away,
The new technology that we now use,
The things you used to hear on the news,
Why do we? Why do we
Take things for granted?

Out with the old, in with the new,
I was always told the future's best,
Oh how I wish the old had never left,
Because all that happens are fights and crimes.
Why did it change?

The guns that are used,
People are accused,
What has this world become since you left?
But we still
Take things for granted,
Why do we? Why do we
Take things for granted?

Kimberly McCluskie (13)
Chalvedon School & Sixth Form College

Racing Generation

As I watch out of the apple of my eye,
Watching all the boy racers go by,
I can see how everything is changing,
Everybody is raging in our world of violence,
Someday it will all just be silence.

Hanna Colman (15)
Chalvedon School & Sixth Form College

My Generation

In my generation there's teenagers all round.
On Saturday we would often hang around the town.
On Sundays we'd laze in and watch TV,
With our mum nagging us to make her tea.
It's not even easy when we go to school,
You've always got to fit in and act all cool.

We may get pressured into anorexia or something we don't like,
Either way, in our time, not everything's alright.
We stress about our hair or worry about growing up,
We want our dreams to come true, with a lot of luck.
Most of us hate our bodies, we're either too skinny or too fat,
So we get all shy and hide under our hats.
I tell my friends not to worry but they say the same back.

I guess we just want reassuring
Because not everything is that bad.
Once we grow up we won't think like we do today,
We will mould into something new like a soft piece of clay.
Worrying won't matter because we'll just be ourselves,
Having built up each year like a tall stack of shelves.

Right now though, we are teens
And we just have to get through our days,
You've just got to live the life you have and don't wish it away.
Being in my generation is hard unless you play it right,
Just keep your head held high and look on the bright side.
You will always have your family and of course your friends,
To help you walk the path you choose, right through to the end.

Kayleigh Bradon (13)
Chalvedon School & Sixth Form College

It's Just People Who We Will Never Know

It's just people who we will never know
All they do is shoot their bullets and go
Defending the country
Isn't that important to you?
I guess not
It's just people who we will never know

People who have wives and children
Grieving because they don't have a dad
A bomb blew him up yesterday
Isn't that sad?
It's just people who we will never know

Little children with guns
Pushing the trigger with their thumbs
Kind men taking pity
I bet they will regret that
When they never return to the city
It's just people who we will never know

So take two minutes
Think about people who we will never know
They are important
Just like you and me
They're not just
People who we will never know.

Sarah Moore (14)
Chalvedon School & Sixth Form College

My Generation Poem

My generation,
I was born in 1993,
I didn't know what my generation
was going to be.

I remember special memories
In my heart, now and then.
Generation is my life cycle,
over and over again.

Everything is changing so fast,
computers, television, iPod and more
inventions have been in my generation.

30 years ago the generation was different from now,
they didn't have all the creations and inventions we've got now.
All persons born about the same time,
that's the start of a generation.

What's my generation like now?
My generation in 2007, there's more technology,
computers, fashion and my childhood's spent at school.
What's the next generation going to be like?

Sarah Ha (14)
Chalvedon School & Sixth Form College

Technology

iPods to listen to,
computers to entertain,
MP3s were made to please,
But, not good in the rain!

MSN and mobiles to chat,
Laptops were made for the go,
Internet to connect,
TVs for watching shows!

Kyna Mott (13)
Chalvedon School & Sixth Form College

My Generation

Like generations before us,
we're misunderstood,
People only see the bad,
never the good.

We're growing up
before our time,
Society sees wearing a hoodie
as a social crime.

Computers are taking over
in everything we do,
Speech is old fashioned,
texting is the new.

Our intelligence is high,
our imagination vivid,
But we drop our hs
which makes out parents livid.

Pollution is high in our generation,
technology is blooming,
With our planet abuse,
global warming is looming.

Jade Alden (14)
Chalvedon School & Sixth Form College

My Generation

Mobiles, computers, TVs,
PC, Xbox, PS3s.

All the music under the sun,
But most people like only one.

While all our troops are in Iraq,
All the kids playing in the park.

Thomas Lines (13)
Chalvedon School & Sixth Form College

A Girl Of My Generation

Hopping off the train with her headphones in,
Nobody knows where she's been.
Last night was a drunken one,
The party was amazing fun!
She'd spent the night in her boyfriend's bed,
And paid the price with a splitting head.
Her parents assumed she stayed with a mate,
Whilst she partied hard and got in a state.
Hungover, she stumbled into school,
Flunked her exams, and felt like a fool.
Just when she got back on track
Her life went spiralling into black.
She called a friend, shocked to the core,
Revealed she's pregnant, and said no more.
A sweet sixteen, turned horribly sour,
Within the space of just one hour.
A feeling of loss returned once more,
As her boyfriend was called to war.
With nowt but an ASBO to her name,
Her life has been a dangerous game.
Like snakes and ladders, there were lows and highs,
But now she's lost, and so; she cries.

Marie Swanson (14)
Chalvedon School & Sixth Form College

My Generation

My generation is young,
Full of drugs and alcohol.
Teenagers drunk and pregnant,
Kids scared to leave their homes.

People on the streets,
Begging for money,
Full of leaders at war.
This is my generation.

Robyn Couch (13)
Chalvedon School & Sixth Form College

Crime Confuses Us

Crimes committed confuse us,
Murder, forgery and assault.
But why do the criminals commit these,
If they know they're gonna get caught?

Why do theses people hurt us
And do things really bad?
Muggings, manslaughter and murder,
Make everyone feel really sad.

The troubles get out of hand,
The police then get involved.
They always try their best
To get the matter resolved.

Bang, goes the cell room door,
Turns the lock and key.
The prisoners keep a tally chart
Till the day that they're set free.

Will this crime century ever end?
Maybe in 100 years.
We need to do something about it
And get rid of all our fears.

Millie Levey (12)
Chalvedon School & Sixth Form College

My Generation

My generation is now,
It is present and to be seen.
It is what goes on around me,
Yesterday, tomorrow and now.

My parent's generation was far back,
People in the future will be then,
But my generation is now,
Yesterday, tomorrow and now!

Annam Mehreen (13)
Chalvedon School & Sixth Form College

Our Life

Is our life set in a certain path,
Or is it a choice, like taking a shower or bath?

Is our life all our own choices,
Or is it a million other voices?

Is our life all our own dreams,
Or is it a feeling like cake or ice cream?

Is our life just up to fate,
Or do we have to participate?

Our life is for us to have some fun,
Like running all day out in the sun.

Our life is all up to us,
Like a choice between walking or taking the bus.

So grab hold of life
Or you will live in strife.

Lucy Hudson (12)
Chalvedon School & Sixth Form College

My Generation

Primary school has come and gone,
That's why I'm singing my song,
Working so hard for my exams,
Soon my GCSEs will fly around.

Rihanna and Chris Brown, top of the charts,
Singing how their lives broke their hearts.
Music makes the world go round,
So jump on board and enjoy the sound.

Sophie Keppel (12)
Chalvedon School & Sixth Form College

My Generation

At the age of ten plus four
I need to know more.

I always ask 'why',
And normally sigh.

When adults keep saying,
'Why do you ask, why?'

Why do I have to be at nine,
When my parents know I am safe and fine?

Why does the washing up have to be done,
When I could be out with my mates having fun?

Why do I have growing pains when I feel fine?
Why do I always have to be on time?

Why do I have to do jobs for my mum,
When I could be out having loads of fun?

Oh why? Why? Why?

Roxanne Bacon (14)
Chalvedon School & Sixth Form College

Football Match

Playing in a football match in the school grounds
While making wild and very strong sounds
The manager having a strictly private conversation
While in a very tricky situation
Whack, whack, the ball goes into the goal
Making the goalkeeper let go of his soul
Sitting there, the manager's really sad
Cheer, cheer, cheer, the crowd goes mad
Winning the match with power up to the max
Now we can collect our money and finally relax.

Mitchell Wright (12)
Chalvedon School & Sixth Form College

My Generation

Computers, games and Internet,
Are all around these days.
All mobiles phones,
Made in lots of different ways.

DVDs all in colour,
Sat navs help you get to your place.
Listen to music on mp3s and iPods,
And arrive there early with a smile on your face.

Kids zooming past
Like shooting stars.
With wheels in their shoes
As they race to their own car.

Tattoos and piercings,
Just hurt a little bit,
But when people start to notice them,
You will never regret it.

Xboxes, PlayStations,
And Nintendo Wiis.
Have fun in the sunny summer sun days,
And have fun with your families.

Jordan Cosburn (13)
Chalvedon School & Sixth Form College

Fashion Poem

Fashion is my passion
Where would we be
If we didn't have fashion?
Maybe we would look as dull as a tree
Skinny jeans have just come in
But yet another style has gone in the bin
All the fashion has a passion
But where would we be without it?

Annalise Aylett (12)
Chalvedon School & Sixth Form College

My Generation Poem

In this world we change from old to new.
Who's next to change something?
It could be you.

From black and white TVs to plasma screens,
Brick phones to thin phones,
An Xbox to a 360.

The generation keeps on changing,
Something must become something new,
So we keep on making.

My generation is for now and ever,
Will it stop?
Never!

Katie Dyas (15)
Chalvedon School & Sixth Form College

Generation Poem

G un crime and danger
E thnicity represented
N o homework should be allowed
E ntertainment and fun
R omeo and Juliet plays and stories
A cting and drama
T elly and movies
I nternet to explore
O ptions to do
N o danger, protection for all.

Channelle George (14)
Chalvedon School & Sixth Form College

My Generation

I like to go out
And hang around with my friends,
We have so much fun,
I don't want it to end.

I go into town
And buy lots of bags,
Then I go home
Holding lots of bags.

I go to school
And see all my friends,
I just can't wait to go home,
I just want the day to end.

Me and my friends
Love to stay out late,
Running around
With a fast heart rate.

I like to go out,
Places far away,
But wherever I go
I'm not going to stay.

I go away
On lots of holidays,
But then I have to come back
To a normal day.

China Benton (15)
Chalvedon School & Sixth Form College

My Generation

A world full of secrets
Secrets never to be told,
A world of love
A world of hate
This is my story of my generation.

A world full of desires,
That we take for granted.
Pumping music through our iPods and mp3s,
A world full of entertainment,
Watching movies through a glass box,
A world full of technology,
This is the story of my generation.

It's not all rainbows and lollipops,
Dark, drugs, danger,
A world full of hate,
Gun crime, knife crime, everything!
All this because of rebellious lives,
Bang!
We all know our lives are on the line,
A world of heartache.
This is the story of my generation.

Farzana Saeed (15)
Chalvedon School & Sixth Form College

My Generation

Generations go on through the magic of time,
Technology moves on getting more complex every year
Older generations were so simple, so easy
Now all is left behind and the old becomes the new.

Mobile phones, satellites, cars and computers
These things have become the new generation
None of these things were known to the older generations
And now we ignore the simple things that bring together the old
and the new
Before using mobile phones, people used to communicate
using letters,
There is no freedom of the fresh air now, only cars exist.

The world has lost the foundations of its past and is covered by the new
No one remembers the oldest days, when kids could run and play
So much crime, so little time
Drags us down and shows us up.

So many expectations bring us to a loose end
As many people lose control
People were happier in the older days
And now everyone is down, as with the weather
The older generation, lost and forgotten!

Ross Adams (14)
Chalvedon School & Sixth Form College

My Generation

Football - a season ticket for two
PSP - a game for me and you

Global warming - take a moment out to think for a bit
TV - what would I do without it

Tax - Robin Hood vs the Government, are they both the same
Terrorists - their aim is to kill and maim

Laptop - surf the Internet with clicks
Cricket - a chance to hit a six

Cars - an advanced mode of transportation
People - make up the population

Pets - a cute, cuddly face to greet you night or day
Money - cash or card, spend it anyway

Xbox 360 - take your brain for a ride
Iraq war - good or bad, you decide

Electricity - switch a button for an electrical flow
Obesity - why let yourself go.

Jack Plane (14)
Chalvedon School & Sixth Form College

My Generation

All the size zeroes, I'm not one.
The streets of London, everyone's carrying a gun.
Technology is progressing so fast,
Arsenal are at the top of the league, how long will it last?
Fergie, Lily Allen, Ne-Yo top the charts,
All singing how their lovers broke their hearts.
Foundation, mascara, lip-gloss, the lot,
Caked onto girls' faces, they think they look hot.
D&G, Versace, the pressure to wear the best,
Life is becoming a stressful test.

Tyrell Taylor-Edwards (13)
Chalvedon School & Sixth Form College

My Generation

The fridge is empty, the cupboard's bare, it's time for a shop.
Any day, day or night, I can shop as long as my plastic's right.
From hats to doormats, pears to garden chairs,
Clothes to computer disks, I'd better make a list.

Jump into the 4x4, foot to the floor, roads are empty by midnight,
Park up quick, no need to pay and display.
Grab a trolley, through the doors,
Wow! It's big, it's a super-mega-store.

Buy, buy, buy, everything will be fine
As long as my credit card survives.
Bleep, bleep, bleep is how the cash till speaks.
Swipe my card, punch in the pin, that's the shopping complete.
Whoops! I forgot the wine,
I'll just go and buy online.

Vincent Taylor (15)
Chalvedon School & Sixth Form College

My Music

The bass of my music
Blastin' really loud,
Boom, boom, the house is shaking.
When Rihanna sings,
Memorised every word,
Singing in the right time,
Skipping to the next song,
Loving what is on.
The songs on my CD,
Make me smile all day,
From the 80s to the 90s,
All the songs are good,
They all remind my dad of his childhood.

Kirsten Mace (13)
Chalvedon School & Sixth Form College

My Generation Poem

Today's world is not the same,
Now it's different, now it's changed.
The new generation and its technology
With consoles and movies and DVDs.
So many laws and so many rules,
Extremists, terrorists and just plain fools.
Wars and fighting and stabbings in parks,
Bullying and hatred and racist remarks.
The way life is it's not for us to choose,
With different lifestyles and stereotypical views.
Where days are boring, so dull and so grey,
With murders more frequent every day.
The good times and thoughts are made up of fake
Because the factors of life really aren't that great.
Living in this time isn't all nice,
This is my generation and this is my life.

James White (14)
Chalvedon School & Sixth Form College

Our War

A fight with a friend,
An argument with a teacher,
Being late for school,
Do a day's work,
Then a pile of homework,
But hey,
There's just one more day,
Till Saturday, 17 November 2007 when I can go and play,
With my friends.

George Smith (12)
Chalvedon School & Sixth Form College

Everything Changes

Older people look down and think we are worse than them
Just because of the clothes we wear
Baggy hoodies
Skinny jeans look like the drainpipe
running down the side of the building.
Everyone in designer things
Nike
Gucci
Ecko
The music we listen to
Isn't like it used to be
R Kelly compared to the Beatles
Is like chalk and cheese
Nothing is the same as it used to be
Everything changes in time.

Charley Grayson (12)
Chalvedon School & Sixth Form College

My Generation

Back in the old days kids would use books,
if we did that now we would get funny looks.
As now there is technology, computers and all,
to help us through our day at school.

Mobile phones for us to communicate,
so many different networks, with all different rates.
iPods, Nintendos, mobile phones and so much more,
these things are said to be so cool, for sure.

Wow! This is 2007!
You really could mistake it for Heaven.

Kirsty Heath (14)
Chalvedon School & Sixth Form College

2007

Here I am in 2007,
I always hear my grandparents say
I live in Heaven,
They say to me they had no fast cars,
They had no PSP, they played with cards.
My dad agrees
And tells me he had to do chores.
Nowadays we worry about getting bored.
Today we have computers, consoles and cable TV,
Some people think we don't really need them
And I agree.
Think of a life where we didn't have these things,
Where we would only rely on health, shelter, food and drink.

Bilaal Romain (14)
Chalvedon School & Sixth Form College

Time Passes

M any things are different,
Y ears have gone by

G randparents have passed
E volution still lasts
N ASA are still going
E verything is still growing
R eligions are more complicated
A nd global warming is serious
T hings aren't normal
I n engaging with people leads to violence
O verall
N othing's ever the same.

Natalie Harmer (14)
Chalvedon School & Sixth Form College

My Generation

My generation, is it better than yours?
Did you have all the different technologies?
Laptops and PlayStations, computers and iPods,
Phones and mp3 players, TVs and DVDs, stereos and Xboxes.
That's not all!

My generation is better than yours!
Entertainment and sports, that's what it is all about.
Bowling and football, cinema and tennis, swimming and rugby,
Discos and cricket, arcades and snooker.
That's just a few!

My generation isn't all good.
Lions, dolphins, whales, elephants, birds,
fish and the Great Barrier Reef,
These all fear extinction.
The polar ice caps are melting, polar bears may die,
The climate is increasing and decreasing all the time.

My generation,
Is it better than yours?
Overall, I think it is!

Shantelle Holmes (14)
Chalvedon School & Sixth Form College

In My Generation

In my generation things have changed
compared to the old 60s and 70s days.
No more platforms and polkadot skirts,
but skinny jeans, Converses and all the works.

In my generation we have
flat screen computers with MSN,
PS3s, 360s and contact lenses
digital cameras and iPods and things that are HD.
Now we can even pause live TV.

Elisha Cunningham (13)
Chalvedon School & Sixth Form College

My Generation

Generation to generation,
Always changing old to new,
I try hard to find an explanation,
Why all things are owned by so few.

Fashion has come on in leaps and bounds,
Designers are trying to find,
Wonderful colours to do the rounds,
Ones that stick in everyone's minds.

Technology has given us things to use,
That years ago were only dreams,
So many things, what will I choose?
Maybe my own, if I can think of some schemes.

Ceri Hopkinson (13)
Chalvedon School & Sixth Form College

The Streets

Walking down the street
Who will you meet?
Don't look up
Stare at your feet.

There they are, standing on the corner,
Another one dead
Only her family mourn her.

Rivalry everywhere
Doesn't anyone care?

Rebecca Taylor (14)
Chalvedon School & Sixth Form College

Talking About My Generation

Talking about my generation
It gives me a memory sensation,
The things I remember,
I'll remember to the end.

Mobile phones and music players, technology,
Fall Out Boy, Panic At The Disco's music,
The things I remember
I'll remember to the end.

Conor Herbing (13)
Chalvedon School & Sixth Form College

Our Generation

Technology is growing
Faster than we're growing ourselves

Scientists discovering cures
For the ill

We thank technology
For the things it can help us with

Our grandparents sometimes
Don't agree with the growing world.

Charlotte Cornwall (15)
Chalvedon School & Sixth Form College

A Day In My Life

I wake up in the morning
I've got to go to school.
So I wash and dry my hair so that it looks cool,
It has to be a certain way, so that I don't look like a fool.
I've programmed my iPod, so I have music in my ear,
Text to my friend to meet, because she lives quite near.
Can't wait till I get home to mine so that I can get back online,
I have a chat with my mate, I have to stop because it's getting late!
I eat dinner, do my homework and get my PJs on,
Go to bed, get some sleep,
Wake up to another day,
And it seems very long.

Chloe McCarthy (13)
Chalvedon School & Sixth Form College

My Generation

My generation
is where we are, not according
but doing instead.
We are not happy,
we are having a giggle.
We are not lying,
we are telling a porky.
We are not chaotic,
we are creating a mess.
I hope you can tell we are different,
Or should I say there is no slang for that!

Robert Duckworth-Coyne (13)
Chalvedon School & Sixth Form College

The Heat's On But The Game's Not Over

As the world heats up, who will be there to save us
From the sheer power of Mother Nature?
And how will we know, or how will we guess
When the Earth is finished playing its best,
And that we're reaching a point where the king is taken,
When the planet will one day cry, 'Checkmate,'
Then, with a crash and bang, we will meet our fate.

Harry Smith (12)
Emerson Park School

Homeless

My family don't want to know me
So I left my home
And my friends
To live on the streets

I am alone and cold
Sitting in a shop doorway
Passers-by give me their loose change
Which pays for my food and water

Life on the streets is hard
You never know what's going to happen
Some people can be kind and give you money
But others just pass by with a look

I am alone and cold
Sitting in a shop doorway
Passers-by give me their loose change
Which pays for my food and water.

Alice Green (13)
Emerson Park School

I Miss

I miss my mum's great shepherd's pie and lovely hugs,
And I miss playing football with my dad,
And I miss staying up late and watching scary movies,
And I miss my rabbit chasing squirrels round the garden,
And I miss my best friend Daniel from football,
We are like brothers,
And I miss playing on my Xbox 360 and Wii,
And I miss my brother playing with me and actually getting on,
And I miss always going round Jack and James' house,
And I miss playing for my football team,
But most of all I miss my family because they're the best family ever.

Kemal Cetinay (11)
Emerson Park School

Education Too Early

Wake up,
The alarm's bleeping,
I think to myself
I'll keep on sleeping.
But I get out of bed,
Better get moving,
Big day ahead,
Can't keep on snoozing.
Check the time,
It's seven-twenty,
I'll sleep some more,
Half an hour's plenty.
But when I wake,
I get the strangest feeling,
I think I'm late!
An idea's appealing . . .
If school started later,
Wouldn't it be easy
To get out of bed,
Without feeling sleazy.

Lewis Shacklady (12)
Emerson Park School

I Miss

I miss my mum and dad's enormous hugs and kisses,
And I miss my mum and dad's tortillas,
And I miss my fluffy, tabby cat climbing up my bed stairs,
Then snoring when he's asleep,
And I miss my privacy in my good, old room,
And I miss my furry, silky, tabby cat
Standing on two feet trying to open the food cupboard,
And I miss my nan and grandad's laughs,
And I miss my trusty old trampoline,
And I miss my TV, watching wrestling for two hours straight,
And I miss my games' table, playing football, table tennis,
Shuffleboard, bowling, table hockey, draughts and pool,
And I miss my nan's scrumptious roast dinner,
And I miss my entire family,

But most of all I miss my freedom!

Jack Quinlan (11)
Emerson Park School

I Miss

I miss the sound of my mum and dad's voices,
And I miss my warm and cosy bed,
And I miss my dad's famous spaghetti Bolognese,
And I miss my mum's goodnight kisses,
And I miss arguing with my brother,
And I miss my baby brother jumping on me
to wake me in the morning,
And I miss my mum and dad,
And I miss my baby cousin Grace, singing,
'Part Of Your World,' from The Little Mermaid,
and I miss going shopping with friends,
but most of all I miss my family.

Molly Jones (11)
Emerson Park School

I Miss

I miss my cosy bed where I can do whatever I like,
And I miss my mum's delicious shepherd's pie,
And I miss my trampoline, where I bounce and jump.
And I miss my dad's angry voice when he gets the hump,
And I miss my bubble baths, which always overflowed,
And I miss my arguments with my brother, 'Yes', 'No', 'Yes', 'No',
And I miss, of course, my laptop which is very slow,
And I miss my lie-ins until about noon,
And I miss my privacy, all locked up in my room,
And I miss my games, which I would play for hours on end,
And I miss my MSN, where I would send messages again and again,
But most of all I miss my family and friends.

Lee Robertson (12)
Emerson Park School

One Chance, One Life

In this world you have one chance, one life
In this world you love your husband or wife
Black or white, it does not matter
You must love and not batter
In this world there are rich and poor
Rich live in mansions and poor live on the floor
People pay for diamonds and pearls
While men are hurting little girls
It's not far, they need a chance
Just think about it, give a glance
Why do people rob and steal?
It's not nice and how would you feel?
People die of starvation
Let's feed the world, feed the nation!

Paul Constable (12)
Emerson Park School

I Miss

I miss my cat, who always wakes me up when I go to sleep
And I miss my cosy, soft bed
And I miss my dad tickling me
And I miss my aunt's home-made curry
And I miss my PSP and playing it
And I miss my mum's hugs
And I miss my baby sister
And I miss my computer
And I miss my home
But most of all I miss my family.

Richard Manton (11)
Emerson Park School

My Secret Garden

I walk into my magical garden
Seeing the sights of mysteries
The wonders that I'm walking past
It's filling me with memories.

That empty, dangling washing line
The sandpit that never got used
The vegetables that never grew
The swing which broke when I was two.

I walk into my magical garden
Seeing the sights of mysteries
The wonders that I'm walking past
It's filling me with memories.

The skip that's full of junk
The climbing frame that's dust and rust
The bike that keeps on beeping
My memories that I am keeping.

Charlotte Brinsmead (12)
Emerson Park School

I Miss

I miss my warm cosy bed, with my thick, pink duvet
And I miss a nice, hot, bubbly bath with my strawberry scented gel
And I miss curling up on the soft sofa, watching Hollyoaks
And I miss cuddling my black, fluffy dog when it's cold
And I miss my jeans and black glitter T-shirt so I can be comfortable
And I miss a good night's sleep in my warm bed
And I miss my mum's really big hugs
And I miss my dad's really bad jokes
And I miss going to Lakeside with my friends at the weekend.

But most of all I miss spending time with my family and having fun.

Grace Levy (11)
Emerson Park School

Being Homeless

Being homeless is such a drag
In fact it's very, very bad
Nothing to eat
Nowhere good to sleep.

People walk past
They stop and stare
And wonder what you're doing sitting there.

Smelly clothes
And no hot baths
Being homeless is not a laugh.

People all assume I'm bad
I just find that very sad.

Oh to have a family
Cosy night in, watching TV
When will I eat again? I don't know
Oh great, the weather looks like snow.

Abigail Dowling (13)
Emerson Park School

Homeless

They sleep in doorways,
No money for food,
Hoping for some change.
Homeless.

Searching through bins,
Looking for something to eat,
Lying there, hopeless.
Homeless.

You see them asleep,
Wondering what went wrong,
So you flick them 20p.
Homeless.

They try for money,
Begging at your feet,
Desperately hoping.
Homeless.

Singing, dancing,
Anything for money,
Standing by their hat.
Homeless.

Sleeping on cardboard boxes,
With a big, husky beard,
They're in for a rough night.
Homeless.

Queuing outside a hotel,
Waiting for a sleeping bag,
A hot meal awaits.
Homeless.

Hot, soapy water,
Washed over their face,
Washing before they eat.
Homeless.

A bed for the night,
In safe surroundings,
You see this is luxury.
Homeless.

Billy Fitzpatrick (14)
Emerson Park School

Homeless And On The Streets

On the streets there's robbers and thugs
Dealing everything, including drugs,
Always hurting the poor and needy
Even when they cry 'feed me'.

Always hungry with nowhere to go,
Through all weathers, including snow,
Once a day we might get fed
But after we're on the ground for a bed.

People kick us, spit and swear,
Others just stop to stand and glare,
We beg for money but in return
People say 'get a job and earn'.

We miss our families, but that's not always the case,
Sometimes we leave without a trace,
I bet it's nice to live in a family home,
Rather than sitting outside all alone.

Elizabeth Chapman (13)
Emerson Park School

My Generation

Our world is changing, rapidly,
Babies being born,
People dying in their place.

Global warming harms us all,
Our generation could be the last,
With people polluting the world.

Our mums and dads
Our nans and grandads
They experienced the same things.

Younger, older and middle-aged,
They all have their own
Generation.

Kate Norris (12)
Emerson Park School

The Homeless Man

A homeless man
Scavenges
In trash barrels
And envies
People who look down on him
With scorn
As they hurry home
To their evening meals.

He crouches
In a rat-infested corner
Content to be with creatures
That don't cringe
At the sight of him.

Jonathan McFarlane (13)
Emerson Park School

Friends

Friends,
everyone needs one, they're always there for you,
when you are depressed,
sad, hurt or happy,
everyone needs one.

They play with you in the sun,
play with you in the wind,
play with you in the rain,
play with you in the snow,
they always put up with you,
even when you're a pain.

They always make you smile,
and they're funny and make you laugh,
especially when you're picked on,
they always cheer you up,
they help sort out your problems,
from Sarah, Jonny or Ron.

So always talk to your friends,
and have fun every single day,
so do the same for them,
cheer them up when they're down too,
go on; be a friend,
because everybody needs one.

Aimée Sell (12)
Emerson Park School

The Homeless Boy

He left home in a pair of jeans,
that he bought in his early teens.
His mum left home when he was four,
his dad took over but they were poor.

He left it and left it, until one day,
he finally said, I'm on my way.
Now he sleeps in a box by a door,
pleading for money for the poor.

The places where he sleeps are cold and damp,
and the police just say, 'Move along you tramp.'
Every day he wants his mum and dad,
and that's his life which is very sad.

George Estcourt(13)
Emerson Park School

As I Sit In The Doorway

As I sit in the doorway,
so hungry and cold,
shivering and shaking,
no blanket to hold.

As I sit in the doorway,
as the wind blows,
I feel so useless,
but nobody knows.

As I sit in the doorway,
watching people go by,
they give me dirty looks
so I start to cry.

As I sit in the doorway,
so frozen and lonely,
I sit here dreaming,
of a place more homely.

Bethany Wells (13)
Emerson Park School

Detention

I shouted and screamed in science class
I wanted all the attention
I didn't realise Miss was watching
So she issued me a detention.

After school on Friday
She shouted in my ear
I tried to forget about it
But Friday's almost here.

It was Friday afternoon
Everyone got to go home
But I was stuck in class
And I was all alone!

The torture finally ended
My mum picked me up from school
Today I learned my lesson
Detention isn't cool!

Tyler Gibbs (12)
Emerson Park School

Friendship

My best friend is kind
My best friend can keep promises
My best friend can keep secrets
My best friend is always there for me.

My best friend is so close to me
My best friend is like the sister I never had
My best friend is with me every day
My best friend is with me day and night.

I wish people had a best friend like mine
I really do wish.

As long as nobody nicks mine!

Toni Murley (12)
Emerson Park School

There Was Once A Young Child

There was once a young child,
left home with ripped up jeans,
been sleeping on the streets,
since his early teens.

There was once a young child,
who lay there in the street,
to every person he's begging,
begging at their feet.

There was once a young child,
not a gold coin in his sight,
for everyone walked past him,
pretending that they're light.

Three was once a young child,
who was finding life rather tough,
with 1 pences, 2 pences, 5 pences,
it just wasn't enough.

There was once a young child,
who needed some food and water,
please someone save this girl,
after all, she is somebody's daughter.

Harry Culham (13)
Emerson Park School

Bullying

Bullying is a crime against humanity
This should not be a reality
This makes the victim sad
So this is very bad
They also end up crying
They may even end up dying

Bullying is very serious
It makes the victims delirious
They don't tell their parents
They get stampeded on like elephants
This should not be done
But the bullies find it fun

Bullies are actually soft inside
'Cause they have a lot to hide
They usually get abused
So they are always confused
When their victims get beaten
Their lunch gets eaten

If you take them head on
The teacher will make them gone.

Jordan Braidwood (12)
Emerson Park School

I Miss

I miss cuddling my pets,
And I miss having a warm shower,
And I miss going out with my loving mum and dad,
And I miss my warm, cosy bed,
And I miss my 52 inch TV,
And I miss my own clothes,
And I miss my PSP,
And I miss my mum's shepherd's pie,
And I miss tackling my dad at football,
And I miss my own, warm room,
And I miss having fights with my brothers and winning,
And I miss my silver PlayStation,
But most of all I miss all of my lovely family.

Connor Squibb (11)
Emerson Park School

Homelessness

Home, home, where are you?
I can't find you

I am on the streets
On a rainy day

Thinking about food
And shelter
When no one cares

When people walk past they
Think I am invisible
Some are afraid of me
And some stare

It's dark now
And everything seems to be quiet
The wind is strong and things are flying about
I sit against the wall thinking about what shall I do today.

Filza Mahmood (13)
Emerson Park School

I Miss

I miss my mum's roast dinner,
And I miss my dad playing football with me,
And I miss falling asleep in the warm, lush, bubbly bath,
And I miss my soft, warm bed,
And I miss my own space,
And I miss my family,
And I miss McDonald's chips,
And I miss my make-up,
And I miss my straighteners,
And I miss my mum and dad's hugs,
And I miss my mum and dad's kisses,
But most of all I miss my mum and dad.

Ellie Constantine (11)
Emerson Park School

Bullying Is Bad

Bullying is bad,
It makes you feel so sad,
It makes people cry,
And makes some want to die.

Bullying is bad,
But victims don't want to tell their dad,
It shouldn't be done,
But that's what bullies think is fun.

Bullying is bad,
Bullies think it makes them a lad,
But bullies are easy to scare,
Only if you dare.

Bullying is bad,
People will think you're mad,
But if you take them on,
Your bullies will be gone.

Matt Brett (12)
Emerson Park School

Friendship Story

Together we have discos, presents and parties,
Toblerone, Galaxy and Smarties,
Always together
Whatever the weather
For ever and ever

Or not . . .

A fight over some water
No longer like mother and daughter
Together forever
Or never and never
Just another row

Or not . . .

Together we go to sleepovers, cinemas and shopping
Skipping, jumping and hopping
Always together
Whatever the weather
For ever and ever.

Laine Swaby (12)
Emerson Park School

My Generation

My generation is great,
There's things I love and things I hate.
Over the park with my best mate,
Coming home to watch Catherine Tate.

In my generation there's lots to say,
Setting up on Saturday for Match Of The Day.
Going to Upton Park, to watch the Hammers play.
I love to spend my weekends that way.

In my generation there's lots to do,
There's lots of things out there for you.
Why don't you try something new,
Like go to the beach or visit the zoo?

In my generation there's lots to see,
Like the new film out on DVD.
My favourite film is Ali G,
Is your opinion different to me?

In my generation there's lots and lots,
Like doing the Gunners at the Emirates.
But then again, there's ifs and buts,
For Zamora to score it took some guts.

Ronnie Scott (12)
Emerson Park School

West Ham United

W e all follow West Ham
E ast London for life!
S melling the aroma of the fast food stands.
T he sweet scents of the freshly cut grass.

H ammers score again!
A victory over Arsenal is hardly surprising.
M anchester United cannot even score against Rob Green.

U nstoppable is the best word to describe Scott Parker.
N oble is 100 percent Hammer through and through.
I nvincible when we play away.
T wo-nil victory over Tottenham.
E therington makes another tackle.
D ean Ashton scores his 25th goal of the season!

Charlie McGinley (13)
Gaynes School

Friends And Family

Family!
Family are so caring,
In everything they do,
They've always taken care of me
And shared a love so true.
They have the sweetest smiles that
There could ever be,
I thank you so much, all of you,
For always loving me!

Friends!
Friends are sort of family,
We have our ups and downs,
We're always back to being friends in the end
And acting like a couple of clowns!

Alice White (12)
Gaynes School

Fairy Tale

Deserted in a school,
They think I'm such a fool,
There's no point for me to cry out,
With no one about.

I need someone to stay with me,
But people leave me be,
Inside, my heart is breaking,
But people think I'm just faking.

I hide my fear,
And put on a smile,
But I know it will
Only stay on for a while.

People don't look at my face,
But they say I'm a waste,
I moan and cry and wail,
But my dream is only a fairy tale.

Elcin Kaya (12)
Gaynes School

My Family

In my family there are four,
They are the four that I adore,
Without them I would be no more.

Fryatts are the ones we are,
Annoying they can be but not all the time.
Marvellous they are all the time.
I am the youngest of all four.
Loveable they will always be.
Yippee, this is the family for me.

Ben Fryatt (12)
Gaynes School

My Generation

As I walk down the street, every day,
This is what I see,
Children playing with attitude, anger too,
Trying to prove how big they can be.
That's my generation.

I turn on the TV, the news is on,
A kid's been shot again,
Violence is spreading, all around,
Causing families grief and pain.
That's my generation.

I'm sitting on the bus as I go to school,
There's some boy sitting in front of me,
He's listening to his mp3 player,
It's so loud you can't hear yourself speak.
That's my generation.

There's a newspaper on the seat beside me,
I pick it up to have a read,
There's a story on the front page, it says,
Another soldier dies fighting for his country.
That's my generation.

Wars should be a thing of the past,
But that isn't the case,
Because all around the world it's happening,
In every kind of race.
That's my generation.

So this is what it's like,
To live in my society,
Violence, attitude, wars as well,
But that's just life to me.
That's my generation.

Abbie Palmer (11)
Gaynes School

My Generation

My generation is the 21st century,
You're probably wondering how people treat me,
But hey, this isn't about me, it's about friends and family,
And all this happens in the 21st century.

The kids, they all play computer games,
They're all addicted, even James.
The adults, those poor, old adults,
They walk around drinking Yakults.

Our weather, the dull, stupid weather,
It rains all day and shines in May.
The schools, the modern day schools,
Built with a spanner, a hammer and more tools.

Our transport, our fast, furious transport,
Watch the red light or you'll get caught.
Our cities, those large, grand cities,
The car showrooms with their tea and biccies.

Our dreams, what have we dreamt?
I can't think of a word that rhymes with this!
I'll tell you what, I'll give it a miss.

I'm sure with this poem
You've been going round the bend,
So here it is -
The end!

Robert Davis (12)
Gaynes School

Talking 'Bout My Generation

Where make-up is overrated,
Where 'boffs' get bullied,
Where you're only 'in the gang' if you fit in,
Where you make practical jokes,
That's talking 'bout my generation.

When everyone boasts about their new game,
When you have to wear the coolest clothes around,
When you must be good at certain things,
When the cool kids don't speak to the 'boffs',
That's talking 'bout my generation.

Where you have to joke to get you out of looking a fool,
Where fake friends back stab,
But real friends are true to you,
Where you can trust a lot of people,
That's talking 'bout my generation.

When you like different styles,
When everyone has a different taste in music,
When people clash,
When people stick together,
That's talking 'bout my generation.

Where you shouldn't talk to strangers,
Where global warming is a big problem,
Where airports have high security,
Where teenagers think it's right to starve themselves,
That's talking 'bout my generation.

Have friends,
Be cool,
Be popular,
But the most important thing is to be yourself,
That's talking 'bout my generation.

Alex Duncan (11)
Gaynes School

My Generation

My generation is an interesting one,
It has goods and bads, plus a heap of fun.
My family and friends are just the best,
But it isn't all happy, so you've probably guessed!

The world is polluted, yes, it's our fault,
But it could get worse as a result.
The blame's on the rubbish we throw away,
Each and every single day!

The park is fantastic, yes, it's great,
But it's the graffiti and damage that I hate.
The swings get broken and I wonder how,
It needs to be sorted, right here and right now!

All on the news is muggings and killings,
They're robbing hundreds and thousands,
Not pennies and shillings!

Now let me tell you a little bit more,
About good times, that are not sour or raw.
Where shall I start, at my school would be good,
As I started in September, and enjoying it as I should.

My favourite subject is PE,
I like to keep fit, it's good for me.
My favourite sport is football,
I would play in goal but I'm much too small!

My interest consist of reading and writing,
If I were a boy, it would be Xbox and fighting.
The music of today is all hip-hop and rap,
The dances and the moves are street dance and tap.

My generation I enjoy, yes I do,
I have fun with my friends and with poems too.
I do my bit to recycle scrap paper,
And when it is done I can relax or just caper!

Holly Peppercorn (11)
Gaynes School

Global Warming

Global warming, global warming,
It's not that boring.
I bet you just think, what the heck,
But you're going to turn the world into a wreck.

Play your PlayStation and use the car,
But why not go out, or walk to the bar?
Why not recycle, it is free,
Because otherwise you will make life hell, for you and me!

The Polar caps will melt, the ozone layer will go,
Nature will have its way and our spirits will be low,
The sun's rays will burn us and all our land,
The trees will perish and animals too,
And no one will be there to give us a helping hand.

Kiran Shah (12)
Gaynes School

My Generation

I'm writing this poem to say,
that us kids of today
are spreading the nation
with Sony PlayStation,
a lot of money the parents do pay.

No time to write down a letter,
we think MSN is far better,
chatting is how we spend our time,
even if the weather is fine.
No interest to us is fresh air,
for that we just don't care.

But to me this poem does not relate,
Although the above I think are great.
I love to spend time with my friends
and have sleepovers at weekends.
See I can't sit still at all,
I'm happiest playing football.

Paige Baker (11)
Gaynes School

Future

In the future you will see
Cars that hover over me.

Planes that fly at the speed of light,
Cutting down the time of flight.

Ships that sail the seven seas,
Powered by the sap from trees.

Trains and buses on time will run,
Powered by the blazing sun.

People working from their homes,
All business done on mobile phones.

Children learning via Internet link,
Never really have to think.

Will it be better? I don't know,
Well, we'll all just have to give it a go.

Alfie Hill (12)
Gaynes School

My Generation

I might not be good at poems,
But I am good at throwing.
So I am going to write about
My generation.

I have a brother, a mother, a nan and a cat,
Believe it or not they don't live in a flat.

My dad is an engineer, my mum a hairdresser
And my brother is a little, messy messer.

I moan a lot, I kind of groan a lot,
That's why I don't stay at home a lot.

Rebecca Barclay
Gaynes School

The Game

The game has started,
Foot and ball have parted,
The players rush in,
Which team will win?

The ball goes out to the wing,
Where the winger does his thing,
He crosses it in,
The crowd make a din.

The defender has committed a foul,
The crowd lets out a mighty howl,
The striker takes his shot,
From the penalty spot.

The shot is a blaster,
But is the keeper faster?
The ball hits the back of the net,
But it's not over yet.

The striker lets rip,
A fantastic back-flip,
The crowd shouts his name,
He's won the game!

Bradley Baylis (12)
Gaynes School

Untitled

The beat was constant,
The banging was loud,
The noise was outrageous,
I couldn't bear the sound.

The drum roll was quick,
As I banged with my stick,
But I guess it's my talent,
It's not just a trick.

The neighbours complained,
They screamed down my ear,
A rush of adrenaline
Flushed away my fear.

I guess it's my life,
It's just who I am,
There's nothing could change it,
Nothing,
Not even close,
But soon it might just have to come
Nearer and nearer to it,
And the decision has been made!

Robbie Walshe (11)
Gaynes School

My Poem

I love to play football out in the park,
With all my mates, we have a good laugh.
We think it's all fun till something goes wrong,
And one of us takes the blame.
I like to play games all day and all night,
And sometimes I get a jolly good fright!
I watch TV until it gets dark,
And I occasionally see the ducks in the park.
When I'm tired I go to bed,
But my parents don't know the dreams in my head.

If I have a nightmare I don't really care,
Because I know it's all make-believe.
When I wake up I brush my teeth and comb my hair,
And sometimes face a grizzly bear!
I get ready for school and a dive in the pool,
Which is usually freezing cold!
You've heard my poem, you know it well,
Maybe one day you'll write one as well?

James Cook (11)
Gaynes School

Sports

S ports keep you fit
P laying increases your knowledge
O ffering some help
R ough rugby gets you dirty
T ackling someone hurts
S haking hands after.

George Cox (12)
Gaynes School

My Life

I hate going out at night,
Because at least one person is having a fight.
They punch and kick,
Then they run away quick,
Before they get nicked by the police.

I don't like going to school,
Cos all the teachers think I'm a fool.
My mates are always in trouble,
Cos they have a little bubble,
But most of the time, they're alright.

I love it when we are off,
Because that's the one time I don't have to boff.
Most of all I love to have time
To party all night,
To the sound of really cool tunes.

Reece Smith (12)
Gaynes School

When I Was . . .

When I was one I learned to walk,
By the time I was two I could really talk,
When three came along I started at school,
By the time I reached four I was really quite tall.
Five followed four, I learnt how to write,
Mum would help me read at night.
Six came next and then I reached seven,
No homework then, I was in Heaven.
When I'd finished with seven I turned eight,
Then nine came along, which I really did hate!
Ten was my best, my school and my friends,
Then along came eleven and it all had to end.
New teachers, new friends,
But at Gaynes I will stay
Till my school days end.

Harry Levy (11)
Gaynes School

My Best Friend

Today I made a friend,
Who's exactly the same as me.
We laugh at others jokes
And act like one big family.

She listens to my dreams,
And listens to how I feel.
But when I'm feeling very sad
We go out for a meal.

She understands what I go through,
And all my wishes and fears.
But she's always there to support me
And we sometimes shed a tear.

I've always tried to let you know,
I'll always be here for you.
And maybe one day
I can support you too.

Well I want to remember this,
Even with our highs and lows.
That we'll be friends till the end
And friends never let go . . .

Megan Warner (12)
Gaynes School

This Generation

There are people around me,
People building flats and houses,
Scientists inventing new inventions
That have never been invented before.
Lots of crimes going on around me,
New creatures being discovered.
Crazy people shouting at me,
Children starting new schools.
Bonfire night and Christmas coming up,
Shopping stores really busy.

Holly Young (11)
Gaynes School

The Sea

Dark, deep and mysterious
Some call it the unknown.
Fast and furious,
The creatures call it their home.
Forever moving,
Never still.
Gives life,
But also can kill.
The greatest power
This world will ever see.
Its beauty, its strength,
The wonder of the sea.
It rages, it roars,
And crashes against the rocks.
The animals scatter,
As it open its jaws.
The waves are like puppies' paws
As they stomp along the sea floor.

Rhys Torris (11)
Gaynes School

Talking 'Bout My Generation

In my generation there's
All gangs and guns.
Knifings round every corner
And
Terrorists with bombs.
Children getting kidnapped
And
Soldiers dying in Iraq
And we are just standing here
Wishing it would go away.

Joe Adams (11)
Gaynes School

A Terrifying Game Of 21 Dares

One day, me and mates
Were playing 21 dares,
Sitting on iron gates,
Giving each other scares.

Looking all around,
Unprepared,
Something on the ground,
I'm scared!

Then some of them ran away,
Leaving me and Bob,
Thinking of something to say,
Trying not to sob.

Looking all around,
Unprepared,
Something on the ground,
Really scared!

Now Bob's decided to go,
I don't want to be alone,
The wind has started to blow,
And I'm sure I heard a moan.

Looking all around,
Unprepared,
Something on the ground,
Ultra scared!

What this game has turned to
Is no longer fun,
I don't know what to do,
I think I should just run.

Looking all around,
Unprepared,
Something on the ground,
Am I scared?

The leaves have all been blown,
To show what's underneath,
It's only a mobile phone,
That has scared me beyond belief!

Sean Thomas (12)
Gaynes School

SLR Pictures

Taking pictures with an SLR,
Is a snazzier hobby I'm sure by far,
Since taking pictures at night with a flash
Makes blinded rats, in the gutter, dash.

Sending the FBI on a wild goose chase,
With blurred pictures of frisbees and a shoelace,
And pictures of slugs depicted in mirrors,
To give the impression of low-lying killers.

The only snag is buying the camera,
£100, £200 or panorama,
Or maybe you would prefer a DSLR,
After all they're simpler, by far.

Thomas Naggs (12)
Gaynes School

Beautiful Game

B rilliant old game of football is so fun!
E leven brilliant superstars vs eleven other brilliant superstars!
A ll of them are absolutely losing.
U nbelievabe, exciting, extraordinary entertainment!
T he best in the world, compete just for fun.
I nvincible, Manchester United win of course.
F antastic, frantic football, such fast action, such action.
U nbeatable, Manchester United, the best, better than the rest.
L eague's all over the world, having fun, playing football.

G ame of football can be played anywhere.
A nytime, park or at a stadium, doesn't matter as long as it's fun.
M e, I play it, I don't get paid unfortunately.
E ven though I don't get paid, I just enjoy it!

Joe Ocuneff (13)
Gaynes School

My Generation

In my generation
There are flat screens
Watching new HD scenes
Footballers costing 35 million
Teams winning, teams losing
Things happening so fast grandparents find it confusing
Mobiles sending and receiving
Technology losing and retrieving
Cars that travel 180 miles per hour
Everything faster, not getting slower
Time to lay down and rest for an hour
Children playing I Spy
Watching from the London Eye
That's my generation.

Cortney Sullivan
Gaynes School

Ross

I like a laugh
I sing in the bath
I like playing tricks
Hardly ever get sick
Ride out on my bike
Until it gets dark
That's me, Ross!

Shopping is boring
PlayStation's king
Rugby is the best
That's the latest thing
To the park for a jog
Whilst playing football with the dog
That's me, Ross!

Ross Lewis (13)
Gaynes School

Shopping

S pending money
H aving a good time
O ff on a roll
P icking up everything that you see
P utting clothes, that don't fit, back
I love to shop till I drop
N othing left in the shops
G oing into every shop!

Abbie Snelling (12)
Gaynes School

The Night World

The grass was green,
The sky was blue,
While I was there
Under the moon.

I lay there awake,
I lay there asleep,
I lay there just like
Little Bo-Peep.

I looked around
And nothing was there,
Just the trees and the wind
Dancing with air.

Nothing seemed close,
Nothing seemed near,
Except for one tiny
Little fear.

And that's when I knew
The night world
Was here.

Hannah Coles (12)
Hall Mead School

Darkness Incarnate

You must love to defeat me
You must hate to strengthen me
You must like to avoid me
You must have greed to find me
I have many names
But am I as evil as they say?
At least it is warm but
I'm just doing my job, punishing the bad
Am I really darkness incarnate?

Jonathan Kesingland (12)
Helena Romanes School

Death

Something that's worse than death
Will certainly take your breath
Remorse is traumatic
Grief's automatic
There's nothing that's worse
Than death.

Josh Burgess (13)
Honywood Community Science School

These Years

Loving the Spice Girls, jelly shoes and Sesame Street,
Those 1990s,
Allowed to run riot, dawn to dusk,
Those 1990s.

Climbing trees to run away from the boys,
Those 1990s,
Pokemon cards were all the rage,
Those 1990s.

Shootings, stabbings and missing children,
These 2000s.
Chavs, emos, gangsters, goths, nerds, grebos,
These 2000s.

Underage drinking and underage smoking,
These 2000s,
Eating disorders and going to rehab is all the rage,
These 2000s.

Global warming, over-polluted,
In the future,
London underwater,
In the future.

Lucy Hall (13)
Honywood Community Science School

Troubled

He doesn't speak out.
His thoughts are bottled up in a tiny corner of his mind.
Permanently crushed by his peers.
Even his friends give him lousy sneers.
He just needs a helping hand on the road to a happy, fun-filled life.
Not downers giving him strife.
When will he get his pick-me-up?
When will he get his time to shine?
Will he break out and be heard,
Or will he withdraw to his bedroom shrine?

He needs to know he's wanted, he needs some love and care.
But nowadays he thinks, *love is all too rare.*
Lonely, troubled, his life is no fair game,
He just wants the world to know his name.
He shouts and cries, he wails and whistles,
But alas, he feels trapped in prison, full of thistles.
His friends and foes, they're too the same,
Out to hurt him, they feel no shame.

Tormented, possessed,
All of the worry is making him stressed.
He needs attention; he needs to be wanted,
Not alone, not destined to wind up dead.
A life of self-harm is not the way,
Then again, he thinks, *what are they gonna say?*
A knife from the kitchen is found,
But then, he drops, right down to the ground.

Luke Jarvis (13)
Honywood Community Science School

An Unexpected Change

Whip! Whip!
Smack! Smack!
The life of an animal at stake,
as again and again,
the whip comes down on my head,
I panicked and tried to run,
But I wasn't as lucky as some.
Eventually it stopped,
then I was forced onto a large lorry,
with no idea of where I was heading,
maybe to my fate,
but no,
as I walked through the market gate,
people standing on a slate.
Then I was dragged out again,
by two big men,
they spoke to me gently,
and patted me on the neck.
I don't remember the journey back.
I came out of the lorry
onto a yard full of horses.
I was put in a stable,
with hay and water.
My life had changed,
now I spend my years happy
in a new home where I am loved.

Imogen Carter (14)
Honywood Community Science School

Global Warming

Ice caps are melting faster than time,
Many boulders of ice disappearing
before I'll be able to finish this rhyme.

The warming of the planet isn't anything new,
Politicians at summits discuss it, but really don't have a clue.

Cut emissions, stop the flying and walk - it's good for the heart,
We all need to act together now and take part.

Cold, bleak winter, summer holidays confused and seasons missed,
Daffodils blooming in the winter, for our future is no longer bliss.

Drought and famine seem to rule our Earth,
Pestilence and disease are on a verge of new birth.

Rainforests no longer have monsoons or rain,
Sea coasts are eroding and we are to blame.

We were given this planet to go forth and enjoy,
But we have ruined man and animals' futures
with an attitude of ignorance we've employed.

Cold summers and hot winters, look at what we've done,
No time for sunbathing - for the weather is no fun!

Packaging and plastic, we just can't get enough,
Our planet is paying the peril of selfishness and sloth.

No more pool parties to look forward to,
As for water, well it's just not going to be new.

From heatwaves to hurricanes, pollution is the link,
At the end of the day, we are the ones on the brink.

People say it's good that we have a year-long tan,
But, for people like us, we're paying taxes for their cancer treatments
and the sun will soon be a ban.

The moral of this story, is to listen, take note,
Don't ignore the fact that you're a contender in this very large boat.

Amy-Jo Miles (14)
Honywood Community Science School

It's Not All Bad

We aren't all bad, it makes us sad,
You were once like us, you know it's true.
Grades go up but our rep goes down,
You think we're naughty when we frown.
You say we're terrible, but look at you,
Bombing, shooting and power-greedy too.
You say we're obsessed with games, phones, MP3s,
But you're the ones that made them and invented these.
We also have fights and argue a lot,
But doesn't every adult lose the plot?
You ask us how our day is . . .
The same every day!
You say we just grunt,
It's like you're on a gossip hunt!
You put programmes on the telly,
Really interesting soaps,
But they always make us feel bad,
You lower our hopes.
If we are big, you make us feel conscious,
And if we're thin you make us feel ugly.
Not everyone looks great,
But it's not all about weight.
There's not much we can do,
And a diet is a no-no!
So don't say that we're bad,
Because we have high expectations,
Just give us a break,
Our lives are not an animation.
Thank you for reading, so now you understand,
And maybe, just maybe, you'll give us a helping hand.

Christopher Ellis (13)
Honywood Community Science School

A Murder In The Snow

Just today I witnessed,
something you'll never know.
I witnessed it today,
as I stepped out in the snow.

A young boy's life has ended,
it's just another day
where another little boy
has wandered out astray.

As I walked around the corner,
I heard a deafening *bang!*
I asked him why he shot the boy
he answered me with slang.

The sights that I have seen today
they just won't ever leave me.
the idea why he killed the boy,
why, it just astounds me.

I stepped into the station
and the officer questioned me,
I very soon discovered
the murderer was called Lee.

As I stood in court,
my anger rose for that boy,
that murderer called Lee
shot him like a toy.

So my message is to you,
the things you have to know,
never, ever kill
anyone in the snow . . .

Katie McCormick (13)
Honywood Community Science School

Insane Addiction

Love, a cruel emotion,
When you break up
It's like a bullet in the heart,
The more you love,
The more it hurts!

Everyday you say, 'I love you.'
But do you ever hear it back?
If no is the answer,
Then what's the point,
Love isn't there anymore!

The harsh reality,
Not just a fantasy,
When you wake up,
The pain is unreal,
You can never love anyone the same again.

But is it a dream,
A nightmare?
Who knows?
The truth is too much to handle,
Wouldn't you like to know though?

The truth could hurt,
Even kill!
It's quite simple, but do you want to hear it?
Can you take it?
Didn't think so!

So the true meaning of love will never be known,
Or will it?

Laura Bailey (13)
Honywood Community Science School

Size Zero - Dying To Be Thin

You see them on the catwalk, magazines and TV
Now, is that stick-thin person
Who you want to be?
They see the skinny models and don't eat for a week,
Carrying on this way when the future's looking bleak.

'Stare at my reflection, I don't like what I see,
I'm dying to be thin, I'm dying to change me.
I don't have a problem, there is nothing wrong,
Stop try to help me,
Just let me belong.'

There's nothing we can do,
There's nothing we can say,
It's a problem in the young girl's head,
It's not going away.
We need to speak out, we need to spread the word,
This problem needs some recognition,
Our voices must be heard.
What does it mean to be so scarily thin.

They're playing a dangerous game
They're never going
To win . . .

Sarah Elliott (13)
Honywood Community Science School

Ribs Poem

When it started it was just a joke
Now I learn I've tagged and provoked,
I've done so much damage, it's hard to believe,
You can't even try to think or conceive.

So much has happened, in such little time,
Everyone knows but they're sour lime.
I paint on a house, I paint on a train,
But to tell anyone, would put me in pain.

People say they do it, so I follow the herd,
And as we were walking I tagged even a bird.
They thought it was funny, they though it was cool,
I even tagged the water in somebody's pool.

Disturbing as it was, I needed a hand,
To stop my mischief throughout this land.
Whoever I went to they would all just laugh,
They should have just killed me, half then half.

Daniel Bradford (13)
Honywood Community Science School

Choices

My head is spinning like a hurricane on go,
I didn't have much, I took it slow,
The migraines I'm having, they hurt so bad,
I've overdosed on paracetamol, I think I'm going mad.

I've never done wrong, I'm a good little child,
My friends said I'd be fine, so I went wild,
It all went so quickly, I didn't get a chance,
It's as if they forced me, and I lost my stance.

If I could turn back time, you bet I would,
But the substance is like prey, it hit me good,
Now I can't stop, I've caught the disease,
I just want help from someone please.

I'm starting to change personality and looks,
You seem to lose both, along in this hook,
My skin's starting to fade, my eyes are starting to droop,
I wish I'd never chosen this route.

Danielle Provan (13)
Honywood Community Science School

Stick-Thin Girls

Stick-thin girls
With their hair in curls
What does it really mean
To be that small?
Not good at all.
It's just a reason to be seen!
Image isn't everything,
Brains, not beauty, is the key.
Make-up, diamonds, fancy dresses
And all these celebrity wannabes!
Who really wants to be like that?
Just step out, take the lead,
Don't be afraid to wear what you want,
Be yourself and you'll succeed!

Hayley Ramsey (14)
Honywood Community Science School

Razor

Jet-leather scalded stones aligned -
Monogamous ellipses.
They glaze your eye and rape your mind.
Psychiatry for gypsies.
Consoled by spectral moonlight milk
Condensed on the slate.
As tear-stained tongues shriek out their lungs
And rusted blood evaporates.

Adapted to unravelling
The edges of your scream.
The umber-furnaced javelin
Shall pierce a childhood dream.
Consigned to desperate scrambling
To sandstone tombs of speech;
To mud-caked corpses rambling
On bedlam's ballroom beach.

Yet spied by theologians;
That procreative lurch -
Fellating newsprint oceans
In the shadow of the church.
A raven, stoned by ecstasy
As wilted doves collide;
Embalmed by smoke ringed lechery,
His razor's blonde deride.

Ciaran Clibbens (15)
King Edward VI Grammar School

My Way Of Life

Why are there world wars?
Why is there no democracy in Iraq?
Too much death and destruction.

Why is there not enough love going around the world?
Not enough happiness,
People have a right to be happy.

Why are some countries so wealthy
And other countries so poor?
Not enough food, too much poverty.

William Freeman (13)
Kingswoode Hoe Special School

Life As A Teenager

When I was a baby I was vulnerable
Because I was helpless

When I was a toddler
I could walk on my own

When I went to school
I made friends

Now I am a teenager
I can take some responsibility
For my life.

Luke Godfrey (13)
Kingswoode Hoe Special School

Life Is Fun As a Teenager

No responsibilities
No worries
Enjoy yourself while you can
I ake care in life
Enjoy your life.

Kieran Richards & Ross Argent (13)
Kingswoode Hoe Special School

More To Life Than Money

There's more to life than money
Because money can't but happiness

Money can't buy love

Money can't buy the world

Money can't buy England

Money can't buy me!

Rhys Quilter (12)
Kingswoode Hoe Special School

Changing The World

Have you ever thought that you
could change the land of
the living?
I want to change the land
of the living to make it a
better place.
I want to save the land
of the living to save the
environment.
I also want to change
the land of the
living in eighty days.
I've been told that
the world is cold.
I want to change the land
of the living but
I've been told that
the world is bad.
To save the environment
the world needs to help.
We need to make the
place better, to make
the world better.

Ranjan Gillati (11)
St Aubyn's School, Woodford Green

An Abandoned Animal

A dog, sitting in the middle of the road, all alone
With no one to play with
Waiting for someone
To take him home
He sees someone
In the distance
His ears fly up and he wags his tail
But they don't take him
He sits down on the floor
And starts to cry
A boy comes
With his mum
The dog runs to him
The boy asks his mum
If he can keep him
She says yes
And the dog finally finds a home.

Hamza Shah (11)
St Aubyn's School, Woodford Green

The Table

Children leaning on my back
and pencils going crack.
People spilling glue
but they always clean up to leave no clue.
My brothers screaming out as they get grazed,
We never stay where we are, it's like being a maze.
Children sticking gum on my sides,
and children always telling lies.
Looking through the window, seeing humans play,
and planes going past, day by day.

Jordan Williams (11)
St Aubyn's School, Woodford Green

The Meaning Of Life

The meaning of life.
Have you ever thought about it?
The meaning of life.

How did it all start?
A question that is unsolved.
Who started it all?

All of us being
Who knows how we began,
The reason we live.

Animals, plants, trees,
Earth, how did it all commence?
. . . the meaning of life.

Zoheb Mirza (11)
St Aubyn's School, Woodford Green

Max The Dog

Max, the dog, wants another life
He hears footsteps, one, two, one, two,
But his heart is cut by a knife,
Footsteps never come his way.

His ears fly up when cars come,
But they always drive by,
Max is always shy.

Harrison Watt (11)
St Aubyn's School, Woodford Green

The One Wish In The World

I wish I could hear everything around me
And hear the sound of people laughing with joy
I could hear my voice, hear my sisters and brothers
But the one wish in the world would be to hear myself sing

In school I can't hear my teacher talk
I can't answer her question or put up my hand
If I can't understand something
But the one wish in the world would be to hear myself sing.

When I see my friends talk and play I feel upset and unwanted
I normally sit alone at break feeling angry with myself
And wishing it was all a dream
But the one wish in the world would be to hear myself sing.

I wish someone could help me, so I could be a normal child
Even though people say I'm normal and I shouldn't think like that
But I know they're lying
But the one wish in the world would be to hear myself sing.

Emel Said (11)
St Aubyn's School, Woodford Green

Soundless

I sit here in my sadness, longing to hear,
But all I can hear is a buzz in my ear.
Sign language tells me it all,
But to hear a voice is what I long for.
I've never known what my own voice sounds like,
But to see joy among people brings a smile to my face,
People don't understand how hard it is,
For a person like me.
All I wish for is . . . to hear.

Rosie Bayliss (11)
St Aubyn's School, Woodford Green

Poor And Alone

I carry pots and strain my back,
I walk around
Bearing a sack,
My feet ache from walking barefoot,
All my clothes are ragged
Torn
And sullied.

I get hot and sweaty
In the blistering heat of the sun,
If I feel sick or ill
I can't just feel better by taking a pill.

I don't know anything about numbers or letters
And my mouth is always dry
And parched.

Yet I can still get on.

Ronique Hossain (11)
St Aubyn's School, Woodford Green

Speechless

The longing to speak goes on and on,
Inside me a fire burns, long and strong,
I'm screaming so loudly but my voice can't be heard,
I want to say how I feel.
When I'm happy and sad,
When I have my evening meal,
The people I see bustling by fast,
Not leaving a care or thought to my wretched past,
The longing to speak goes on and on,
Inside me a fire burns, long and strong.

Manisha Doal (11)
St Aubyn's School, Woodford Green

Through The Eyes Of Fire

I rip up houses
It's easy, like snapping a stick.
I make people scream
At the mention of me.
Animals flee
At the sight of me.
They are weak compared to me.
I am Fire!

Alexander Tudor (11)
St Aubyn's School, Woodford Green

My Weather Poem

My happiness is white, falling snow
Landing on the green, glossy grass.

My love is the red, falling and rising
Sun, balancing in the sky.

My jealousy is the transparent, cold carrying frost
Lying on a bed of concrete.

My anger is the blue, jumping sleet
On the top of dirty roofs.

My shyness is the silver, dancing hailstones
In my mind.

My curiosity is the black, scattering rain
On my skin.

The weather is like a TV
Always changing its channels.

My pride is like a new bird
Who has learnt how to fly.

Liam Reynolds (12)
The John Bramston School & Sixth Form College

Art

Paintings, pictures we draw together
For ever and ever, I could do this forever
Paint on my fingers, paint on my toes
I have paint on me from my head to my toe
Splash, splash, on the paper, I love to draw
Then splatter on the floor, the water's on the door
The joy and happiness of painting me
It's just so fun, I need a wee
I love painting flowers, it's the best
So much better than all the rest
I have to go now, it's lesson time
I can't wait to come back tomorrow and
Mess up again!

Leigh-Anne Nial (11)
The John Bramston School & Sixth Form College

Untitled

War is black
Loneliness of a dark room.

War is blue,
Sadness of a soldier's tears.

War is black
Frightening as dark smoke.

War is yellow
Frustration leaves marks on men

War is a red angry blanket of blood.

Troi Briggs (13)
The John Bramston School & Sixth Form College

January, February, March, April, May - Oh You Get The Point

January is a month of the year,
A month of the year, a month for cheer,
January is a month for things
Like cute little dogs and sparkly rings.

February is a month of the year
A month of the year, a month for cheer,
February is a month of course
For light purple and a seahorse.

March is a month of the year,
A month of the year, a month for cheer,
March is a month of the hare,
So do beware the foxes' lair.

April is a month of the year,
A month of the year, a month for cheer,
April is for Harry Potter,
Pale green and an otter.

May is a month of the year,
A month of the year, a month for cheer,
May is for a nice, blue sky,
Emerald green and butterfly.

June is a month of the year,
A month of the year, a month for cheer,
June is the month for a dig,
Pale pink and maybe a pig!

July is a month of the year,
A month of the year, a month for cheer,
July is a month to stop coughing,
And to start liking turquoise and beautiful dolphins.

August is a month of the year,
A month of the year, a month for cheer,
August is a time for love,
And lots of letters sent by a dove.

September is a month of the year,
A month of the year, a month for cheer,
September is the start of a new path,
And time to think of a long-necked giraffe!

October is a month of the year,
A month of the year, a month for cheer,
October is so lovely,
With light blue and a husky

November is a month of the year,
A month of the year, a month for cheer,
November isn't time for fear,
Guy Fawkes is nowhere near.

December is a month of the year,
A month of the year, a month for cheer,
December is a time to care,
For a cute, white, polar bear!

Maisie Greenwood (11)
The John Bramston School & Sixth Form College

It's Dark And Dangerous

It's dark and lonely
The slippery, scary serpent, slides across the grass.
It's dark and dangerous.

The scary owl's eyes, wide awake,
Looking for its prey,
It's dark and dangerous.

Birds flying like aeroplanes,
Foxes watching your every move,
It's dark and dangerous.

It's light and people have been woken up,
The birds are singing and everyone's dancing,
It's light and safe.

Adeayo Banjo (12)
The John Bramston School & Sixth Form College

The Weather

My love is so red for the sun,
so I can sunbathe on the beach.
My cloud is so green,
raging to let the sun come out,
moving here and moving there.
My ice is so grey, it makes me sad,
because the ice is stopping me playing.
My rain is blue,
Like the tears you cry,
My fog is red, anger black and grey.
The weather is good and bad
Like people's behaviour.

The weather!
The weather is good and bad
Like people's behaviour.

Diane Norris (12)
The John Bramston School & Sixth Form College

Emotions

My happy ball of sun is pink
Moving across the Earth
My upset wind is yellow
Running from car to car.

My sad piece of black,
Lightning running across the sky
My curious moon is gold
Jumping from star to star.

My anger is clouds of blue
Rain running through my head
My love is fog and purple mist
Jumping in the air.

Lewis Newlove (12)
The John Bramston School & Sixth Form College

The Weather In Me

My grey, cloudy, thoughtfulness
Jumped to my mouth like a kangaroo.

My red-hot, heated, hatred
Ran like a cheetah running through the jungle.

My golden lightning hope
Skipped like a skipping girl.

My light blue despair
Jagged like a leaf, whizzing past on the ground.

My pure, white, snowy happiness
Hopped along like a rabbit in a field.

My dark blue, misty sadness
Whizzed past like an eagle in the air.

Jack Cutts (12)
The John Bramston School & Sixth Form College

Flowers

Flowers are pretty and colourful,
They're springy, sprungy and tall.
They're shining all the time
From the big burning ball.

Flowers are soft and gentle,
Their stems are tall and straight,
They're ready for the birds and bees,
To help them pollinate.

Some flowers are tall and small,
Some are tall and big,
They're all round and colourful
And smell rather sweet.

Yasmine Smith
The John Bramston School & Sixth Form College

The Sea

The sea is a vast stretch of water,
That carries on for miles and miles.
The sun shines on it, reflecting blues and greens.
All is quiet on the sea,
Waves lapping gently in the breeze,
Bobbing and bucking, swish, swoosh, swish.

Boats fishing in the early morning,
Casting their lines,
Their reels sounding in the quiet air,
Phwishshsh, phwishshsh, phwishshsh.

Boats bounce in the sea as they catch the fish,
Dolphins dive downwards deeply

Groups of fish swim in the sea,
Darting about like a firework display,
Then regrouping as though they are one with the sea.

As the wind picks up,
Driftwood dances on the sea,
Swaying to the sea's music.

All is quiet tonight on the sea,
The fish sleep, the boats are moored,
The waves are calm and the sun goes down
Like a ball that's been burst.

Elliott Newell (12)
The John Bramston School & Sixth Form College

Winter

Cold, cold, cold.
My breath freezes in the air
My hands go all numb
Crack, crack, crack
The skidding ice breaks
As I tread wearily across it
Cold, cold, cold.

Harry Waldie (11)
The John Bramston School & Sixth Form College

The Sea

I look out as far as my eye can see
White foam bubbling around my bare feet
I feel the spray of the ocean on my face
Soggy, slimy, cold, wet seaweed entwines around my feet
Like an octopus clinging to its prey
The sea's temperament changes in the blink of an eye
I know he's angry because the waves are getting stronger
Forcing the foam up into the air
It crashes, bashes and lashes onto the beach
sending it hurtling towards me
like a pack of white wolves
more than ready for a meal!
I stumble backwards with my feet sinking fast
Losing my balance, I'm captured, surrounded by sea
It retreats as fast, with speed, dragging everything with it
I'm freezing, freezing, freezing, but not ready to be recaptured
I stumble to my feet backwards
Not ready to enter its den.

Taylor Jones (12)
The John Bramston School & Sixth Form College

Emotion

My anger is lightning of red, stamping across my mind.
My joy is a sun of yellow, dancing around me.
My pride is a cloud of gold, parading itself around me.
My hate is a vortex of maroon, spinning around me.
My depression is white, like snow, dragging itself around me.
The weather is a mix like a one pound mix-up.
The weather is like colours, beautiful in their own way.

John Matthews (12)
The John Bramston School & Sixth Form College

Emotional Plant

My petals
My petals are sad and selfish,
They use up all the sunlight and won't share it.
They close up at night and open in the morning
Tall and bright.
My petals are bright, bubbly bundles of joy
They dance like ballerinas in the breeze
And the pollen makes people sneeze!

My leaves
My leaves are happy and healthy, like an Olympic runner.
They are sometimes upset, but never in summer.

My stalk
My stalk stands firm in the wind.
It is serious, sensible and strong,
And very, very long.

My roots
My roots are anxious and angry
Hidden under the soil - dreary and dark
Amongst the stones and bark.
My roots are naughty and nice
They twist and they turn in the ground
Turning around and around.

Emily Smith (11)
The John Bramston School & Sixth Form College

Emotions

My desire is a cloud of orange dancing in the air,
My envy is a beam of lightning that stomps all over me,
My cheekiness is falling raindrops singing higher and higher,
My love is a tornado spinning around, not knowing where to go,
My depression is snow dropping, getting colder and colder,
My hurt is spikes of hail, growing and growing.

My emotions are still not knowing.

Jody Morris (12)
The John Bramston School & Sixth Form College

Emotional Flower Poem

My flower is like a tall giraffe,
My flower is happy as a star in the sky,
My flower is like a shooting star,
My flower is full of joy.

My flower smells like perfume,
My flower has colourful petals,
My flower is like a dancer,
My flower is like a hot, shiny sun.

My flower has green, soft leaves,
My flower is like a roaring rocket,
My flower is a shiny diamond,
My flower is like a crystal of love.

My flower has loads of love,
My flower sometimes feels sad,
My flower is like a red rose,
My flower is a powerful thing.

My flower is going to say goodbye,
My flower is going to have a good life,
My flower feels very happy.

Lucy Pike (11)
The John Bramston School & Sixth Form College

My Weather

My anger is a piece of red lightning
My love is a pink heart
My scaredness is like a grey mouse running from a cat
My sadness is a light blue drop of rain
My happiness is a moon full of joy
My curiosity is a white cloud floating along
My desire is a piece of snow rolling along
My jealousy is a black piece of sleet
My weather is like my mood, forever changing.

Sam Smith
The John Bramston School & Sixth Form College

Autumn Is . . .

Autumn is a time to walk,
kicking leaves up in the air.
Red, brown and orange,
they dance without a care.
Autumn is summer's last breath,
the sun setting low in the sky.
Birds gather on trees high above,
wings spread and ready to fly.
Swoosh, swish, down from the sky,
the auburn leaves start to fall.
Swish, swoosh, high above them
the bare trees are left standing tall.
Falling down slowly,
they land one by one.
Winter is just around the corner,
and autumn is almost done.
Conkers on the leafy floor,
children picking them up fast.
This must be my favourite season,
such a shame it does not last.
A multicoloured carpet,
sleeping on the ground.
Crunching, crackling underfoot,
almost a magical sound.
The autumn must soon give way
to winter's icy chill.
I'll have to wait another year
for autumn's leafy thrill.

Charlotte Wilson (11)
The John Bramston School & Sixth Form College

The Sea

The sea is crashing, smashing, dashing waves,
Along the bobbing shore.
The sea is a cool, still pool, left by the tide,
Swimming shrimps galore.

The sea is an army of angry white horses,
Like creatures running amok,
The sea is the treasure of shimmering shells,
Clustered on slippery rock.

The sea is a shoal of glimmering fish,
Darting through the foam,
The sea is a world of mystery,
For many a watery home.

Alec Willett (11)
The John Bramston School & Sixth Form College

My Brace

Oh, to wear this brace,
this brace upon my face,
Each day I look in the mirror
I remember the things of nice taste
like chocolate bars, boiled sweets and
chewy bubblegum.

I remember the taste of the sweetness,
yum-yum, in my tum.
But I know it's for my own good
the two years will fly by
My teeth will be all nice and straight
and I'll get all the cute, fit guys.

Kerry Hasler (11)
The John Bramston School & Sixth Form College

My Emotions

My multicoloured love thumps through my body like a blood rush.
My yellow skies of happiness drift past me as the moon sets.
My lonely transparent rain flickers on the side of my cheek,
like a leaking pipe.
My silver, aggressive lightning crashes on the ground,
like a bouncy ball.
My shiny jealousy is like sleet bouncing off the floor.
My gold moon triggers me with its beaming light of honesty.
My blue tornado of curiosity spins round me like a spinning top.

Rebecca Franklin
The John Bramston School & Sixth Form College

Emotional Flower Poem

The sunshine is on my happy face,
My petals glow, full of grace,
My leaves float in the wind,
Taking in the oxygen.

My roots burrow into the earth,
Sucking the goodness for all it's worth,
To make my stem big and strong,
So I can grow far and long!

The bumblebees come and go,
To take the pollen to and fro,
To spread my joy as they go.

Laura Newlove
The John Bramston School & Sixth Form College

The Sea

I stand and wait for the sea to visit me.
I stand on the sun-baked sand,
I see the white horses coming towards me.
They look angry and restless,
the anger is reflected in their pale faces.
I stand and wait, the sea is crashing and bashing
against the rickety rocks.
The sun soon starts to settle down
and so do the white horses.
They calm down and settle by my feet.
The sun has gone down,
I am surrounded by water,
it's beckoning me with its hand.
I run as far as I can,
but I'm being called into its land.

Shannon Barrett (11)
The John Bramston School & Sixth Form College

Flowers

My petals are as colourful
as the rainbow.
My green, long stem is
as tall as a skyscraper.
My brown, stringy roots are as
thin as a worm.
My green leaves are
as soft as feathers.
My petals are as small
as twinkling stars.

Leigh-Anne Weller
The John Bramston School & Sixth Form College

Friends

Make-up, miniskirts
Are what my friends wear.
I let them get on with it
Cos I do not care.

They all wear their make-up
Especially for school.
I think it's kind of weird
But they think it's cool.

I've now found some new friends,
Who are my true mates.
Best friends forever,
That's what this poem states.

Chloe Humphreys
The John Bramston School & Sixth Form College

My Generation

S o many say we're bad,
T oo many people are afraid.
E veryone thinks we're yobs.
R eally have the wrong facts.
E very day we are slated.
O ver things we didn't do.
T eenagers are really quite polite.
Y oung people are not rude.
P eople have the wrong impression.
E ven we hate yobs too.

Zack McGuinness (13)
The Sanders Draper School

Wasteful

When you are in a circle of crime
there is no getting out
you are out of time
you are in doubt

now you're in court
you look at the jury
your lesson is about to be taught
they look at you with fury

now you're in prison
you have nowhere to go
your time has run out
your life is over.

Michael Buckland (13)
The Sanders Draper School

Teenagers

T eens are not all yobs or hooligans.
E veryone should be treated the same.
E ven if there are some troublemakers.
N ot everyone is the same!
A lot of teenagers just act troublesome.
G et a kick out of feeling big.
E ven though there are a lot, wouldn't you
R ather give us the benefit of the doubt.
S tupid teens are ruining our reputation,
    but don't treat us all like those stupid teens.

Mitchell Webb (13)
The Sanders Draper School

My Generation

M y generation
b y Elliot Barker

g un crime
e vil
k n ives are being carried, stained by innocent blood
e nd of life
r acism
a nger fills hearts with hatred
t ime goes by
i ntent to kill
o n the streets
n o one is safe

This poem explains our heartfelt sorrow
But I wonder
Will I live to see tomorrow?

Elliot Barker (13)
The Sanders Draper School

Teenagers

T he media never has anything good to say about us
E veryone thinks we are yobs
E veryone misinterprets our behaviour
N o one thinks our behaviour is acceptable
A criminal offence we have not committed
G ood behaviour some of us have
E veryone hates the sight of us
R un riot and cause havoc, not all of us do
S ee us all as individuals.

George Goodey (13)
The Sanders Draper School

My Generation And How We're Portrayed

My generation is portrayed in a bad way
Everyone just listens to what the media say
We're always being accused of carrying knives
But have they stopped and thought, they are ruining our lives?

Nobody ever thinks about their teens
They just stop and judge and think we're all mean
Some of us are different
Some of us are right
But nobody cares
We're always in the spotlight

We're trying to change
We're making it light
But with all this pressure
Who knows what's right.

Rebecca Willats (14)
The Sanders Draper School

Our Generation

Fashion and music in 2007,
The people in England, they're in Heaven.
Modern technology, electricity too,
Lots of people, there are quite a few.
Grungers and goths,
Chavs and boffs,
Gangsters and normals,
People dressing formal

Our generation!

Chloe Smith (13)
The Sanders Draper School

Teenage Lies

Get drunk, get drugged,
Anyone with money, mug.
Stone cars, smash door,
Any litter on the floor.

All the media does is lie,
To them being a teenager is a crime.

Just stab or slash,
Police are coming, I'll just dash,
Shoplift, get money,
All my mates think it's funny.

All the media does is lie,
To them being a teenager is a crime.

Make gangs, fight now,
All because we had a row,
Have drugs, get tested,
Oh my God! I've been arrested.

All the media does is lie,
To them being a teenager is a crime.

Jack Turton (14)
The Sanders Draper School

Teenagers

T eens have started to join gangs
E ven some teens have started taking drugs
E veryone should be treated equally
N ot everyone is causing trouble
A lot of teens are not involved in gangs
G angs are one of the biggest problems
E veryone should try to stay out of trouble
R ather than taking drugs
S ome people need to get a life!

Lauren Thomas (13)
The Sanders Draper School

My Generation

My generation,
Your expectation.
Those Monday mornings,
All those yawnings.
The week passes,
We have had all those classes.
A Saturday night
Gives people a fright.
Hanging with friends,
Have to go in when the day ends.
You see those bad boy faces in all those places.
The police tut,
As we wipe the blood from our cut.
Everyone should be treated the same,
Even though some people are plain.
By plain, I mean people are lame.
The weekend is over,
Back to school,
Great! More people trying to be cool.

Rosie Bailey (13)
The Sanders Draper School

My Generation

Kids of today
Are going down, they say.
Smoking fags at ten,
Shoplifting at eleven,
Taking drugs at twelve,
Pregnant at thirteen,
Bunking school at fourteen,
Getting arrested at fifteen,
Shot dead by sixteen.

Kaffy Ayofe (13)
The Sanders Draper School

My Generation

I've always liked music since I was a child,
But now it's time to set my life wild!
I love to dance around the house,
Mum says I move like I've seen a mouse!
Clothes shopping is what I love,
Buying winter clothes now - hat, scarf and gloves.
You go into a shop and the music is loud,
I walk around with my head in a cloud.
Then in the shop my favourite song comes on,
I turn around and my friends have gone.
Bobbing around I don't want to leave,
My friends are back, one, two, they heave!
Now in the shopping arcade a glittery dress catches my eye,
I walk into the shop, it's gorgeous, what a great buy!
Bags very heavy, we head for the bus stop,
Passing the cleaner with her bucket and mop.
I flake out on the settee when I get home,
An idea pops into my head - on goes my music, as I hear Mum moan!

Kirsty Mills (12)
The Sanders Draper School

My Generation

My generation is creative and cool,
Without us there is no one to go to school.
My generation is fun and smart,
Without my generation there's no end or start.

To us they abuse, judge and criticise,
It's time for the whole world to realise,
We're funny, we're cool, we're certainly not formal
But life without us just wouldn't be normal.

We don't like people to underestimate us,
Yes, we're noisy and naughty and cause lots of fuss.
The children and adults make up the creation,
The world cannot be without my generation.

Belmira Okoro (11)
The Sanders Draper School

When The Young Gangs Meet

When the young gangs meet
In the cold feeling of hate
When the young gangs meet
For everyone it's just too late

When the young gangs meet
With their guns locked and loaded
When the young gangs meet
The calm atmosphere has exploded

When the young gangs meet
With the stench of death around them
When the young gangs meet
It's the last one alive and it's a problem

The last young gangster looks around
His life is over, he's taken the bait
When the young gangs meet
They've locked their fate . . .

Tom McGovern (14)
The Sanders Draper School

My Generation

T is for truancy, we are not guilty.
E is for education, we need this.
E is for energy, we use it up!
N is for naughty, don't blame us all.
A is for angry, elders always shouting.
G is for gangs, not all have guns.
E is for enjoy, have fun with friends.
R is for rules, they should be followed.
S is for stubborn kids, they're not interested!

Danielle Thomas (13)
The Sanders Draper School

My Generation

The GCSE grades are up
The behaviour is down
An eleven-year-old was shot
Now violence is all around

Knives are being carried
Kids wearing hoodies
This generation's meant to be smarter
But we're playing on PSPs

We have mobile phones
And go on MSN
Football players are worth millions
Some kids even have a den

14-year-olds are smoking
A twelve-year-old is pregnant
Her dad thinks she's joking

The ice caps are melting
Floods across Britain
Kids get a good pelting
Into rehab goes another litt'un

Now it's rock and pop
50 Cent and Razorlight
It used to be Status Quo
And karaoke on Friday night

This generation is bright
It can change the planet today
But people's views remain stubborn
Kids are good, not just to get in the way.

Ross Woolward (12)
The Sanders Draper School

My Generation

M ost people's behaviour is good
Y oung people are considered bad

G CSE grades are at an all-time high
E ven though they don't matter to some
N o one can tell what they'll get
E veryone at least tries their best
R iots caused by meddling kids
A ll of us scared stiff
T eachers saying their goodbyes
I t's time to go on and get a job
O pportunity arrives for the students to start their lives
N ow it's time for the Year 7s to arrive.

Michael Wilson (12)
The Sanders Draper School

My Generation

M y generation is full of crime
Y et nothing is done

G etting worse and worse
E veryone getting a bad name
N eed something to sort it out
E lders are getting scared
R owing out on the streets
A ttracting attention
T o cause another row or fight
I wish reality was safer
O thers can enjoy themselves
N ot worrying.

Sophie Furlong (12)
The Sanders Draper School

My Generation

M y generation may not be the best,
Y et it is good enough for us,

G oing through hardships with friends and family,
E ven though people mess about on the bus.
N ew technology always coming in,
E veryone getting excited, showing off their stuff.
R eally, a lot of people are not understanding life,
A ctually they're not that tough.
T eachers trying to teach young children,
I n reality, kids don't really care about what they say.
O n Sundays, you lie at home and do what you want,
N obody actually cares about their day.

But who said that was about me?

Maxine Nhin (12)
The Sanders Draper School

My Generation

Pregnant 16-year-olds with no guts to tell,
They try telling the father,
But he says, 'What the hell!'

You're getting bad grades, but you don't care,
All boys really want is spiked-up hair.

You have drugs to get you high,
Your parents ask what you're doing, but you just lie.

You're bunking school, with your mates,
Running around the field and climbing over the gates.

Well, by the way, that will never be me,
You're killing your future, don't you see?

Jayne Hardy (12)
The Sanders Draper School

My Generation

M oaning, everyone keeps moaning at us!
Y elling at us is all some people do.

G angs are around because there's nothing to do
E veryone thinks we are all criminals
N ot everyone hangs around on the streets
E veryone thinks we don't deserve any respect
R arely are we praised for the good things that we do
A ngry with people blaming all of us
T omorrow we'll all be bored again
I solated from older people
O bviously some of us are criminals, but not everyone
N o one treats us for who we are.

Lydia Butler (13)
The Sanders Draper School

My Generation

T aking drugs and smoking
H aving fights in the street
E veryone accuses us of things not done

R obbing shops, using guns
E veryone is not the same
A ll of us should just play nice games
L ooking around at us, in the street

U nderstanding us is the key
S top accusing us, *let us free!*

Ashley Burdett (13)
The Sanders Draper School

My Generation

My generation have no respect, they say,
We're the adults of tomorrow, but we're the children of today.
Adults forget us, neglect us, show no respect to us,
They put us under so much stress, to always do our very best.

And even though we're forgotten, we daren't make a fuss,
Because then the media will spread lies about us.
According to them, we're murderers, thieves, liars,
And even hooligans, who like to start fires.

But they forget about how clever we are,
We have manners and dreams to go far.
But no matter how much we try to make adults see,
They'll never realise they used to be like me.

Brooke Cooper (12)
The Sanders Draper School

My Generation

What has become of young people?
They are in a bad light more than the limelight.
They've landed in the deep pool.
Gun crime, stabbing, this is not what *we* do at night.
You haven't heard our other side.
It really isn't that bad.
It's not like everyone died
And I reassure you it's not that agonisingly sad.
So I tell you the good part,
More and more passing GCSEs,
Well, it's got be a start.
It's better than getting police fees.
For now, the future is fight,
Not bright.

Govinda Tiwari (12)
The Sanders Draper School

My Generation

My generation is plummeting down,
The rudeness makes the elderly frown.
People work for more and more money,
But the world is getting more and more sunny.

Gun crime raids the streets,
Along with murderers, liars and cheats.
Lots of peer pressure at school,
Kids these days think knives are cool.

Reduce, reuse, recycle they say,
Does anyone listen though? No way!
The world's resources are running out,
But girls today just want to pout.

But shall we end with a good thing to say?
GCSE grades are beyond delay.
Britain's academic levels are high,
My generation makes me sigh.

Samantha Harris (12)
The Sanders Draper School

My Generation

GCSE results higher than ever,
Us children are getting more and more clever.
However, gun crime is increasingly high,
More and more children are going to die.
Children taking knives to school,
Just cos they think that it's cool.
Smoking fags and who knows what?
Cocaine, marijuana and even pot.

Sophie Reynolds (12)
The Sanders Draper School

My Generation

My generation
The people of today
'Look at those hooligans,
On the street corner,' they say.
Alcohol at 12,
Smoking at 13,
Drugs at 14,
Shoplifting at 15,
Pregnant at 16.

The older generation,
'No respect,' they say
What is there to do,
Where is there to play?
This is all we have to do,
This is today.

Dianne Apen-Sadler (12)
The Sanders Draper School

My Generation

We are teenagers now,
But our lives have just begun
And I'm writing about
How we're portrayed by everyone.

Vandals and scumbags,
Are how we are seen.
You see,
This is what I mean.

We're not all like that,
Trust me.
I see.
Have *you* seen the results of our GCSEs.

Michael Wilks (12)
The Sanders Draper School

My Generation

Our school results are flying,
while other teenagers are dying.
17 teenagers killed since May,
while my school results are hitting As.

Football is hitting other heights,
while kids hang about on corners, waiting for fights.
Steven Gerrard is playing great,
but Rhys Jones is another late great.

Bullying nowadays is even bigger,
people that do it will be working a digger.
Some kids will get good jobs,
others will be getting caught by cops.

The world is changing,
that is what I've told you in this letter.
Hopefully, it will be changing
for the better!

Keenan O'Sullivan (12)
The Sanders Draper School

My Generation

Roses are red, violets are blue, look at me bad
And I'm gonna shoot you.
That's all you hear every day,
Even teachers are wearing bulletproof vests.
That's what they say.
Cos now people are getting shot every day,
Now they say, 'Better shut up, or you're going to pay.'
Meanwhile GCSE grades are getting better.
Bang! Bang! Gunshots make people even more scared.
Stuff is good at school,
But outside school people can be cruel.

Vincent Abifarin (12)
The Sanders Draper School

It's Funny

It's funny how we get cursed
It's funny that we are always wrong
It's funny how we don't think straight
It's funny that most of us get carried away in a hearse.

It's funny how we're always shooting
It's funny that we're always stalking
It's funny how we're always the ones to blame
It's funny how most of us don't have a clue what's going on.

But it's brave how we still get there.

It's brave that we get on with our lives
It's brave how we don't give in to the bad ones
It's brave that some of us are still decent
It's brave that some of us stand up for our rights
It's brave that some of us go day to day trying to give us a good name.

AK Meheux (12)
The Sanders Draper School

My Generation

On the bus, on the way home from school,
Children are rude, they're acting fools.
They get off the bus, pull up their hoods,
Fully armed, they set off into the woods.

An old man, who cannot see,
Is in the street begging for mercy,
But no, the youngsters just walk by,
Without even a tear in their eye.

Girls and boys go out in gangs,
Warning people with gun bangs.
Why can't our generation see,
That this is not reality!

Georgina Edwards (12)
The Sanders Draper School

My Generation

They think we're trouble, they think we're crime,
The government's running out of time.
To find a medicine to cure us.
They think we're a disease, poisoning blood,
Lurking on street corners, hiding in mud.
Sometimes I wonder if they'll ever see,
Kids laughing and giggling happily.
When grannies and bus drivers give us rough looks, treat us like dirt,
Make us hurt,
There's not a care in the world about how we feel,
To them everything's perfect, when we're quiet and still.

Sacha Edelman (12)
The Sanders Draper School

Wouldn't It Be Great

Wouldn't it be great if the world didn't end.
No murders or burglary to send police round the bend.

Wouldn't it be great if there was a cure for the blind
And all teenagers would be really kind.

Wouldn't it be great if there was no litter on the ground,
There would be more pretty flowers all around.

Wouldn't it be great if there was no such thing as drugs,
So there would be no more thugs.

Wouldn't it be great if we made use of time and space,
And so the world would be a better place.

Rebecca Stokes (11)
The Sanders Draper School

My Generation

My generation . . .
Mostly full of intimidation.
The situation in the nation,
Teenagers bored and get a bad idea,
Exaggeration form the media.
Stopping out till midnight,
Doing terrible things,
Because there's no light
To see a clearer sight.
Even adults get scared,
And even the old, young and innocent.
Stabbing, shootings, everyday,
Was someone's life taken today or even yesterday?
Police get shot, just because they are securing the country.
Other teenagers are taking a chance and are up to no good.
Media is full of bad news,
Innocent people getting confused, about exaggeration.
What is the future holding for the nation?

Adedolapo Shangobiyi (12)
The Sanders Draper School

My Generation

M y generation
Y our generation

G uns are on the streets
E veryone's hanging around
N ot everyone's nice
E ven in the day, it's still scary
R anting and raving every night
A re you afraid?
T he stabbings and shootings will never end
I t's my generation
O ld people are scared
N o one likes it.

Harley Sultana (12)
The Sanders Draper School

My Generation

Some of our generation's test results are flying
But some of our generation are dying.
Being stabbed and being shot,
While the others have got A stars, As, Bs and Cs,
These people are being rewarded with Xbox 360s.

Racism is a dreadful act,
That is a well known fact,
Saying horrible things about each other,
Saying bad things about the other person's mother.
Enough about the bad,
Time for some good.
Just remember that we have hope,
Don't lose it
And together we can make a better world.

Christopher Secular & Robert Lamacraft (12)
The Sanders Draper School

My Generation

M aybe we could change
Y outh crime and safety

G iven the chance
E veryone could change
N ever say never
E verybody's life could change
R ight down to the last person
A t least it could get better
T ime is of the essence, crime needs to stop
I n the future will it be better?
O nly we can change our life
N o one knows what will happen next . . .

Lindsey Moran (12)
The Sanders Draper School

My Generation

We are young and we are still kids.
We don't know what is right and wrong.
Even though we are young,
Adults don't realise it.
Many think we are bad,
But they don't know the truth.
They imagine we are bad,
Just by looking at us,
But they don't know the truth.
What do they think of the bad kids?
Do people think they are good?
Some do, but some don't,
But they don't know the truth.
Or do they?
Not all of us are bad, some are good.
Why do people think we are bad?
We are the new generation,
We are not that bad.
Every year our GCSE results boost up,
So why do people think we are bad?
We are the new generation and we work very hard.
We are the new kids,
Who care about others.

Alisha Oommen (12)
The Sanders Draper School

Dark Days

I lay there on the cold, hard floor.
Frozen from head to toe with a little, icy nose.
I see snow start to fall, I sneeze, 1, 2, 3 . . .
I huddle up to keep warm then,
I start to fall, I see a light,
And then I'm woken by a cop,
And I move along.

Joe Butler (11)
The Sanders Draper School

If I Could Change The World

If I could change the world
Everything would be perfect

There would be no homework,
But don't stop there, no school, *yes!*

There would be no robbers
And we would all be rich!

But there is more:
No fighting
No jail
No killing
No tidying up
No paying
No arguing.

But best of all, we will all be friends!

Mikah Ruthven (11)
The Sanders Draper School

My Generation

Our generation is good
But we don't do what we should
You wouldn't see me with a gun
Or stealing a car for some fun
To carry a knife
Or take someone's life
It's just not me
In reality
This life of crime
This dreaded time
Is my generation.

Edward Sawyer (12)
The Sanders Draper School

Talking About My Generation

Just because we're wearing hoodies and skulls,
while sitting on the bus,
the all the oldies begin to make a fuss.
We're not even talking loudly,
but the older people start calling us rowdy.
One of our mates tell a joke,
we all burst out laughing at the bloke.
The people tut and shake their heads,
now we all wish we stayed at home, tucked up in our beds.
We all stand up for our stop,
my friend asks me where to shop.
As a group we jump off laughing,
ready to buy chips, we end up halfing.
The bus driver sighs with relief,
passengers roll their eyes at us in disbelief.
People think just because we're kids,
we're lazy troublemakers a load of ids.
When really we're just having fun,
nothing more, no harm done.
People judge, way too fast,
how long is this going to last?

Tori Smith (11)
The Sanders Draper School

My Generation

My generation is a chump,
People killing and people thumped.
Everything's wrong,
And families have gone.
I wonder what is coming along . . .

Oliver Muldoon (13)
The Sanders Draper School

A Lonely Dog

Why did my owner go and flee?
Why couldn't she learn to look after me?
Why couldn't she come back another day?
Why instead did she leave here in dismay?

I want her here, I want her now,
I don't know why she couldn't learn how.
I am feeling really confused,
I am really not very amused.

Come back to me, I silently cry,
Come on, come back, oh why, oh why?
Come back and let me free,
Come back and watch me simply be.

It all happened so suddenly,
It made me smile happily,
It was on Monday when she came,
It was a promise it wouldn't happen again!

Annie Boxer (11)
The Sanders Draper School

My Glorious World

Take me somewhere I can breathe,
No more pollution,
Just happy scenes.

Take me somewhere I can see
Flying birds and honeybees.

Take me somewhere I can hear
Children playing with loving care.

Take me somewhere where I can show
Wild berries when they grow.

Shana Francis (11)
The Sanders Draper School

My Generation

My generation is intellectual and unique
We are educated and wise, with top GCSEs
In sports and athletics we shine bright
And I'll prove that I am right.

Growing up in this period, how hard do you think it is,
Where everything is criticised despite its good qualities?
Never do you praise us for our achievement,
Even go as far as to say that people give us no easy treatment.

But remember the example that you are setting
Lighting the path which we will be following
Pain and destruction, war and anguish
Is that what you want us to be, is that your wish?

But as in human nature, all of us can't be perfect
Some of us are spoilt and some are derailed
But you must realise that picking on them is the media's process
To make their viewer ratings progress.

So now you tell me, what do you think,
After hearing the story from the side that we link?
I don't think our life is fair and that we are free
I hope that I have been able to make you agree with me.

Mehleen Brishti (12)
The Sanders Draper School

My Generation

My generation is a tip,
People hurting and killing,
Knives are bad, guns are worse,
People mugging for a purse.

My generation couldn't get worse.

George Munns (12)
The Sanders Draper School

My Generation

When the media talks about us
They always make us look bad.
They accuse all of us of being bad.
They never give us a good word,
The media has betrayed us.
Not all of us are bad,
OK, some of us do what the media says,
But not all of us.

If we had more to do,
The police would have less to do,
If we had more to do,
The media would have less to say.
Now the government needs to give us more to do.

Most of us do good,
We are the new people of the Earth.
Most of us do well at school,
Not all of us are a fool.
We are individuals,
Don't treat us as if we are all bad.

When we are with our friends,
It doesn't mean we are there for trouble,
We are trying to be social.
Politics, old people, media and police,
Give us a bad name.

Why can't they give us a break?
Police give us ASBOs.
Old people moan
Politicians haven't got a clue
And the media
Well the list would go on and on about them
We have a name
But it's out of date!

Alexander Massart (13)
The Sanders Draper School

Changing The World

C ars cause pollution,
H ave some shame,
A ll of us think it's a game,
N one of us want the blame,
G oing on around the world,
 I t's so scary,
N ot knowing what's going on,
G ive and take is at an end.

T oo many greenhouse gases,
H armful things kill our planet,
E veryone panicking.

W e can stop it,
O r we'll die,
R eally special,
 L ovely fresh air,
D efinitely, killing the Earth!

Steven Weatherley (11)
The Sanders Draper School

Dreams

In my dreams,
I long to be,
With that someone, just him and me
Strolling along hand in hand
Dodging waves that caress the sand.

Then my mum shouts, 'Get out of bed!'
And just like that my dream is dead.

I can't wait until I fall asleep tonight,
When I hope my dream is of the exact same sight.
And that someone fills my dream with laughter
And I find my happy ever after.

Gracie-Lee Johnson (13)
The Sweyne Park School

Dreams

In dreams I can forget my fears
Live in a world with no sorrows or tears
In dreams my life is what I want it to be
I can do what I want, go places I long to see

In my dreams I can soar on the highest cloud
Not pressured to make anyone else happy or proud
In my dreams I can swim in the deepest sea
Not worrying about anyone else except me

In dreams I can be surrounded by those who I love
Or flying solo in the peaceful sky above
In dreams I'm a hero who's honoured and brave
Maybe tonight I'll save a village from a tidal wave

In my dreams my imagination is set free
I escape the horrors of the world around me
In my dreams there are no catches, hooks or conditions, but . . .
After those precious eight hours, I have to wake up.

Sarah-Jane Riley (13)
The Sweyne Park School

Dreams

Dreams, dreams, dreams
Sometimes they can be good, sometimes bad
There are daydreams and sleepy dreams,
Wishing dreams and scary dreams.
Dreams can make you feel like you are floating.
Dreams can make you feel like you are falling.
Some dreams you wake up from and you're swimming in sweat.
Some dreams you sleep the whole night through without waking up.
There are dreams where you have them and in the morning you've
forgotten them.
I like the dreams which are scary and haunted.
Dreams.

Tom Gains (13)
The Sweyne Park School

Dreams

Dreams, dreams I don't understand
I tried to take reality in the palm of my hand
Tonight and tomorrow, what is the theme?
Nightmare, nice or an ordinary dream?

I see a dead body, I stare and freeze
But then I turn hot despite the winter breeze
The blood rolls to my feet like a river or stream
That's all I can say about my nightmare dream

Dreams, dreams I don't understand
I tried to take reality in the palm of my hand
Tonight and tomorrow, what is the theme?
Nightmare, nice or an ordinary dream?

I'm happy floating in the air
Nothing else matters, total despair
No guns, no war, no sight of a knife
Maybe for one time only I'm happy in this life

Dreams, dreams I don't understand
I tried to take reality in the palm of my hand
Tonight and tomorrow, what is the theme?
Nightmare, nice or an ordinary dream?

Riley Lovegrove (12)
The Sweyne Park School

Dream Poem

Have you had a dream that made you think twice?
Dreams are so sweet when the outcome is nice.
Or maybe a nightmare that has made you scream?
Maybe you woke up saying it's just a dream.
All dreams mean different things,
Maybe today you'll dream of your findings.

Sophie Miles (11)
The Sweyne Park School

Dream Poem

I had a dream
If I had a big dream,
I would walk to the moon and back by rocket.
If I had a small dream, I would go to America for 4 weeks.

I had a dream,
If I had a big dream
I would own my own zoo because I love animals,
If I had a small dream, I would own my own farm.

I had a dream,
If I had a big dream,
I would destroy all the people that start wars,
If I had a small dream I would have all the money in the world.

I had a dream,
If I had a big dream,
I would end world hunger,
If only a small dream could be to have world peace.

Kieran Long (13)
The Sweyne Park School

I Dream

I have a dream,
No pain, no danger,
And the world will be a brighter place,
So I can shop till I drop,
I hope that I don't grow old,
I hope so much that it will come true.

Hannah Brown (11)
The Sweyne Park School

A Dream . . .

A dream is conceived in different ways,
As wishes or visions that can last for days,
They can be about people, dogs or cows
But no one quite knows why or how . . .

A dream can be remembered,
A dream can get away,
But if you have a dreamcatcher
They'll stay for another day

A dream can be inspiring,
Makes you want to achieve,
More than you ever thought
And you never want to leave

But one night . . .

Everything turns nasty,
Everything turns red,
You see the Devil's boiling pot
He's ready to be fed

The Devil's tail is red
He's standing by your bed
You want to get away
But you know that's not the way

What about the dreamcatcher?

Your favourite dream starts to appear
The Devil and his pot disappear
Chocolate dogs and the fair!

Isobelle Hollington (13)
The Sweyne Park School

Dreams

When the city is no longer light,
The sun has gone down and said goodnight.
Peace fills the chilly air telling us it's time for bed,
To shut our eyes, to rest our head.

We fall asleep and dream of things,
Of hidden lands where flowers sing.
The sun shines brightly and whistles all day,
The oak wood trees in dark forests sway.

Though beyond the hills things start to unfold,
The sun disappears, the breeze goes cold.
With every step shadows bring,
Fear and darkness to everything.

When the city is no longer light,
The sun has gone down and said goodnight.
We fall asleep and start to dream,
Things are no longer what they seem.

Chloe Muchmore (11)
The Sweyne Park School

Dream

To dream you use imagination,
Finding worlds of your creation.

What you want is what you get,
I'm sure that you will not forget.

In dreams you get all types of creatures,
Some can have quite scary features.

Some dreams can be fun and exciting,
Others can be dull and frightening.

To dream you need to close your eyes,
Or maybe look up to the skies.

Sweet dreams.

Hannah Beeching (11)
The Sweyne Park School

Dreams

Dreams can be very funny,
Dreams can be sad.
Sometimes they are very good,
Sometimes they are bad.

I dreamt I was a footballer,
I was captain of the team,
But as I kicked the ball real hard
I woke up from my dream.
Instead of kicking a football
I'd kicked the dog instead
And a big white ball of fur went flying off the bed!

I dreamt that I was hungry,
I was eating a marshmallow,
But instead of eating a fluffy sweet
I was munching on my pillow!

I dreamt I was a rock star,
I was lead singer of the band,
Until a demented rock fan
Chopped off my playing hand.
I hit him with my guitar,
I was in such a rage,
But he turned into a zombie,
And chased me round the stage!

Elliot Easton (14)
The Sweyne Park School

Dream

I have a dream that one day
all the people in the world sign for peace
and that everyone is happy forever.

I have a dream that one day
all the people in the world agree on no more wars
and that guns don't exist.
I wish that we will all be safe.

Alex Hanrahan (11)
The Sweyne Park School

In My Dreams

In my dreams,
I see a place,
Where I can be wild and daring and free.

Where the butterflies are stirring,
The waterfall is churning,
And the whole world revolves around me.

Flowers blooming,
Swaying gently in the breeze,
Bluebells and warm buttercups

But then, there's the alarm,
And I stop feeling calm,
Oh why do I have to wake up?

Emma Paterson (13)
The Sweyne Park School

The Annoying Thing

The annoying thing looks just like me,
vivid blonde hair,
wild and free.

Our interests are quite the same,
we both desire eternal fame,
me as an astronaut, him as a chef,
it's totally identity theft!

It's really quite obvious,
but you mightn't have guessed,
the reason our lives are the same,
linked and pressed,
the annoying thing's
my twin!

Rachel Hudson (14)
The Sweyne Park School

Dream Dancer

I went into a dream last night
Thinking it was my own
How can it be, that it is not?
I thought to myself alone.

But then I noticed something strange
Something not quite right
It wasn't like my other dreams
And it gave me quite a fright.

A man was standing next to me
But he wasn't there before
I wished him away silently
Hoping he would be there no more.

I opened my eyes and there I saw
The man with a wide smile
He said, 'Do you not like me, little girl?
I shall stay here for a while.'

I thought about my mum
Her voice inside my head
I wanted to get out
So I pinched myself instead.

I woke up to a nice surprise
Green grass on the floor
Although this was not my bedroom
It was an improvement to before.

And then I saw him once again
Dancing round the trees
I asked him to let me go
He just said, 'Say please.'

Beckie Thomas (12)
The Sweyne Park School

Dreams

Zzz!
Off to sleep,
After counting a couple of sheep,
Abstract as dreams can be,
Should I go and sail the sea,
Or will I be like Peter Pan,
Or will I meet Superman?
Could I see?
Could I be?
Let the dream unfold for me,
Should I swim, should I fly?
Over the chimneys and up sky high,
Down below I see the lights,
Flying in the dark sky night,
If only my life could be a dream,
Imagine how surreal life would seem,
Then I land and sit and stare,
Looking at the moon up there, somewhere,
I fall asleep in a dream,
And wake up with a change of theme,
With a bright green sky and an eerie feel,
And got up with the urge to kill,
With a blink I change back to life,
Without the urge to grab a knife,
I'm clueless, thoughtless,
More or less useless,
Where do we go from here?
Who knows?
That's the beauty of a dream!

Josh Jervis (13)
The Sweyne Park School

My Dream

In my dream I dreamt I would stop poverty around the world
Stopping all violence and aggression in sight
I dreamt I met the Queen and we had tea and biscuits together
Chatting about all sorts of imaginative things
What did you dream?

I also dreamt I was in a magical world with all the animals
Safe from extinction and selfish poachers
I dreamt about wars finally being halted to a stop
No more fighting at last
But what did you dream?

Lastly I dreamt of having some money for myself
Just as a little treat
I hope my dream comes true
As it would be amazing to see
For now I just sleep in peace.

Katie Watkins (14)
The Sweyne Park School

Dream Poem

I have a dream that people will not pollute the Earth.
I have a dream that people will not do drugs or anything that will hurt
their bodies.
I have a dream that people will not hurt or kill other people because
they feel like it or just for fun.
I have a dream that you will dream these same things, just like I do.
So don't be afraid to dream.

I have a dream that one day everyone will live in peace.
That no one will be left out of games because of their skin colour,
But because of their ability in the game.
Everyone should have the same rights.

Michael Vann (13)
The Sweyne Park School

Dreams, Dreams, Dreams

Dreaming safely in my bed,
With the pillow to my head.
Feeling safe and peaceful, all alone,
No words, no sounds, not even a phone.

In my house so quiet, so sound,
But in my head, a new world I have found.
Your imagination is free when you're asleep,
But you're calm and silent, without a peep.

You can be a rich millionaire,
Or a boy or girl who gets a huge scare.
Anything is possible, joy or fear,
Your friend, your mum or a monster can appear.

Dreams are magical in every way,
In the way of the picture or the things people say.
Everything's fine or at least it seems,
When you're asleep and your head's full of dreams.

Aaron Baker (11)
The Sweyne Park School

Dreams

I have a dream, a big dream of world peace
I have a dream, a small dream of no homework
I have a dream, a big dream of no poverty
I have a dream, a small dream of free money

I have a dream, a big dream of no global warming
I have a dream, a small dream of being famous
I have a dream, a big dream of no pollution
I have a dream, a small dream of my team winning the FA

I have a dream, a big dream that everyone is equal
I have a dream, a small dream of being a famous cricketer
I have a dream, a big dream of new inventions
I have a dream, a small dream of shorter car and plane journeys.

Martin Winter
The Sweyne Park School

Dream Poem

I wake up in a dark, dull room,
My eyes are blurry, my sight faint.
I see the grey clouds pacing upon the sky,
My eyes darken away.

The door opens,
No one's there,
I stand up
And my head starts to whirl.

I hate the scene outside,
Silent, not a single sound.
As I look around, I question
'Where am I?' the answer isn't given.

Suddenly, I realise it's a dream.
I wake up in a bright, colourful room
And see the real me.

However, I don't remember my dream anymore,
No thoughts come across my head.
I'm somehow quiet and shy,
I recognise myself getting darker than ever.

Monica Gurung (13)
The Sweyne Park School

Dreams!

D eep in sleep, I dream of my future
R eality seems so far away
E ternity is how long they take
A ll ideas of déjà vu seem impossible
M any involve flight or sunny destinations
S trange creatures attack in my nightmares.

Kerry Moorby (13)
The Sweyne Park School

Dreams

A fairy-tale wedding, a date with a star,
A big house, or a flash sports car,
A nice time away with family and friends,
I just hope that the dream never ends.

A fine time relaxing, in a little rowing boat,
Or live in a castle, with its turrets and moat,
Be a famous fashion model, and follow the latest trends,
I just hope that the dream never ends.

Explore the creatures, of the magical wood,
See the path, where Hansel and Gretel stood,
A summer of sun, would be a godsend,
I just hope that the dream never ends.

A field full of flowers, the beautiful smell,
Live in a mansion, with a swirling stairwell,
A fresh cup of coffee, the finest of blends,
I just hope that the dream never ends.

Lauren Forsyth (13)
The Sweyne Park School

Dream

She always met me with a smile,
She made each day worthwhile.
She never spoke but I always knew,
My love of her was so true.

I'll never forget that horrible day,
The day that her love for me went away.

I'll always remember her face and hair so long,
And the way she cruelly said, 'Dream on.'

She was a dream come true,
Until she became a horrible nightmare!

Emma Green (13)
The Sweyne Park School

The Dream Catcher

As the sun sets over the house and trees
I close my window to shut out the breeze.
I shut my eyes, wanting sleep to come
And before I know it, the dreams have begun.

Laying on a Hawaiian beach
Palm trees flapping in the soft, soft breeze
Music playing in the background
And the waves are dancing in the sea.

And then it changes . . .

I'm on my bike, cycling the fastest,
Winning the Tour de France.
Smiling at the cheering crowd,
Feeling triumph in my heart.

And then it changes . . .

Smiling broadly at the audience,
I toss my hair and start to dance
Step, twirl and point
I'm ready to take the chance
So I leap

And then it changes . . .

I'm in a haunted mansion
Cobwebs scattered everywhere,
Floorboards creaking as I step
Ghosts looking around for something to scare
I feel a tap on my shoulder
And I turn around and hear someone say
'Kapow!'

The dream catcher saves the day!

Maddie Scates (11)
The Sweyne Park School

Dreams

Shining with light,
Shrouded in dark,
Your mind is dreaming
Jumping with sparks.

It can be a bliss
Full of joy and fun,
Or a menace in the dark,
Making you want to run.

Happiness, sadness, sorrow and joy,
A dream is meant to be enjoyed,
Based on the past and things to come,
The meaning known by only one.

Your eyes slowly open,
You begin to forget,
Is this world real?
Have I awoke? Not just yet.
I'm pulled back in,
My dream not yet done,
I'm awoken too early,
My eyes wait for the sun.

The ringing and beeping,
The noise that I dread,
The noisy alarm clock going off by my bed.
The snooze button once,
I drift off once more
And slowly but surely in dream world again.

Shining with light,
Shrouded in dark
The world is asleep
And jumping with sparks.

Beki Humm (14)
The Sweyne Park School

The Painful Dream

Spain is a hot and sunny country
Home to that amazing thing
But who knew that it
Was home to the biggest bull ring.

Crowds are cheering
Babies are screaming
The camera flash
Sends the stadium beaming.

Until silence rings out
The ring is clear
The creature enters
The ringleader is near.

A girl in the crowd is the only one not cheering
She is confused
Until she gets very upset
When the bull is abused.

Bashing and thumping
He's thrown through the air
People are chanting
Without a care.

The ringleader laughs
Looking deep in the bull's eyes
Seeing how scared he is
Looking beneath the hungry flies.

However, he just doesn't care
A spear goes through its thigh
Then another one
And a man yells, 'Aim high!'

The bull is helpless
He is not in the wild
He is petrified
Like a lost child.

He falls to the ground
There is a loud scream
It is the young girl
She is me, and then I wake up from this painful dream.

Jade Stockwell (13)
The Sweyne Park School

My Poem Of Dreams

I have a dream,
A big, big dream,
A dream of no starvation,
A dream of no hunger,
A dream of no famine,
I wish this dream could be true.

I have a dream,
A little, little dream,
Just for me,
A dream of a feast,
A dream of lots of food,
A dream of a big treat,
I wish this dream could be true.

I have a dream,
Another big, big dream,
A dream of no fear,
A dream of no illness,
A dream of no death,
I wish this dream could be true.

I have a dream,
Another little, little dream,
Just for me,
A dream of riches,
A dream of health,
A dream of long life,
I hope this dream comes true!

May all your dreams be happy!

Lauren Annette (11)
The Sweyne Park School

It's Only A Dream!

The more I dream,
The more I seem
To be drowned in a dream.

I thought I saw a butterfly,
Still asleep, I flew high.
I wanted to stay like this forever,
To fly away from the winter's weather.
I wanted to fly to southern Spain, the Sahara Desert
Or the African Plains,
Jump on a spaceship to Timbuktu,
Visit a volcano or an American zoo.

I could be anybody, anyone I like,
I could be a lion or married to Mike.
I could be a dog chewing a bone,
Or I could be somebody who wants to go home.
Get out of my nightmare,
Get out of my dream,
It all seems real but it's only a dream.

Sophie Glasson (13)
The Sweyne Park School

Sleeping On Dreams

Sleeping on dreams, lying on a bed,
Sleeping on dreams, it's all in your head,
Tossing and turning, all night long,
What type of dream is right or wrong?
Is it where you float in the air,
Or is it something that gives you a scare?
You wake in the morning refreshed with no care,
Remember or forget, your dream was still there,
What was your dream sleeping on?

Fay Oxby (11)
The Sweyne Park School

I Have A Dream

I have a dream
a dream of life
where nobody dies
I have a dream
a dream of Arsenal
winning the Premier League

I have a dream
a dream of no wars
where we don't lose lives
I have a dream
a dream of having a Ferrari
speeding along a dusty road

I have a dream
a dream of peace and harmony
where we all like one another
I have a dream
a dream of winning the cricket World Cup
where I get praised

I have a dream
a dream of changing climate change
to make the environment better,
but my most important dream
is that everyone has a good life
and goes to Heaven for it.

Liam Bond (12)
The Sweyne Park School

Dreams

I dream to play for England one day,
Running around and playing on a Sunday,
Dreaming of the best things ever,
Seems to go on forever,
Hoping that I won't have a nightmare
That will give me a scare.

Ryan Tierney (13)
The Sweyne Park School

Dreaming

The moon danced merrily across the dark night sky
The sun has gone down the hours flew by
I shut my eyes tight and think with a grin
What a comfortable bed I'm in!
I sail across the sky, the ground at my feet
What a wonderful dream, so many people to greet
I dance with the mermaids, see aliens and boats
I visit huge castles with dragons and moats
I fly with the birds and wave to the trees
See beautiful flowers and big bumblebees
Imagine the stars, so beautifully drawn
They are the flowers on a big black lawn
I love to dream, the hours fly by
The night is soon over
To the moon it's goodbye
What a wonderful night
To dream and to gaze
No more mythical creatures, no seas or no maze
Until tonight my new found friends
I can't wait until dream time
Until the day ends!

Alexandra Smith (14)
The Sweyne Park School

My Dream

I have a dream, a dream of peace and no wars,
but I also have a dream of a black Lamborghini.

I have a dream, a dream of no pollution
and no global warming;
I also have a dream of being rich.

I have a dream of no cutting down trees.
I dream of no terrorists and bombs.
I also have a dream of having a private jet.

Callum Pearce (11)
The Sweyne Park School

Dreams

I have a dream,
That one day I will be rich, not living in a ditch,
Healthy and wise too.

I have a dream,
To be funny around my school
And for the teachers to think I'm funny too.
To at least get an A in my test.

I have a dream,
To win the Euromillions,
To be on television,
All over the world.
I have a dream!
I have a dream that there will be no school days.

Harry Hannigan (13)
The Sweyne Park School

Dream

I have a dream,
A dream of peace,
People would always be friends,
That arguments never existed,
No war had entered the world
And that death was never planned.

But I have another dream,
A dream of a chocolate world,
Milk, dark and white,
All kinds of chocolate,
My fantasy world,
My heaven!

Alexandra Roberts (11)
The Sweyne Park School

My Strange Dream

If I go to bed, I will fall asleep.
But if I fall asleep, it will happen again.
Bright lights will shine and the whispering starts
And I find myself at the windowpane.

I can't really make out what I see in the distance
But the wind, it calls my name
And then I'm floating on a cotton cloud
Somehow, I know the way.

I'm carried off high in the darkness of night
But there's a bright light shining - I feel no fright.
It's really peaceful, but I still hear the sound
Of whispering somethings and it's all around.

And then I stop, climb off the cloud
I've travelled so far but this looks like home.
I take a look around for some clues that just might help
But this is empty, feels scary and I want to yelp.

I open my mouth but nothing comes out
I'm in a world of silence, but I want to get out.
This doesn't feel right, it doesn't feel good
I need to leave, I wish I could.

I turn around to take a look
But there's nothing to see - nothing in sight.
Why can't I lead a normal life?
Instead of strange dreams every night.

I wonder if I will ever know
What it is I never did see
I guess tonight, I might find out
When I revisit my very strange dream.

Emily Houillon (11)
The Sweyne Park School

Dream

A dream, a dream is what I do best,
I think and think and then have a rest.
Sleeping, making and cooking all day,
And then at the end I get a good pay.

Sleeping and sleeping all day long,
In my dreams I sing a song.
A song with lyrics, music and beat,
And now all I need is something to eat.

A piece of chocolate, fruit or cake,
Or apple pie, I could make.
All I need is a rolling pin,
For the apples slices to go in.

Making and making every day,
Food or cards all this way.
Birthday, Easter or Christmas,
Pizza, spaghetti or couscous.

I love to make, build and cook,
Watching TV and reading a book.
To help me get good ideas,
And listen with both my ears.

Cooking and cooking most of the time,
Mixing vegetables with red wine.
Smell, taste, feel and see,
All goes well with a cup of tea.

Served on a plate is horseradish and mustard,
With ice cream and some custard.
This meal sounds great, but not together,
I hope this dream lasts forever.

Catherine Burling (13)
The Sweyne Park School

A Little Chocolate World

It is a nice summer's day in Cocoa Town,
and everything is a scrumptious brown,
I walk along licking my lips with glee,
as this is my dream with no one to share,
all this wonderful chocolate is all for me.

There are chocolate houses and a chocolate school
and even a chocolate-filled swimming pool!
There are chocolate flowers and chocolate trees
and tiny chocolate bumblebees.

I'm in Heaven as chocolate is my favourite treat,
24/7 all I can eat,
Chocolate buttons, Smarties and cake,
From this dream I hope I never wake!

Emma Farrow (11)
The Sweyne Park School

Dream

Everything's been different
All the day long,
Lovely things have happened
And nothing has gone wrong.

Nobody has told me off,
Everyone's smiled,
Isn't it great,
To be a birthday child.

This very special day
Come once every year,
So take the opportunity,
Have a party and cheer!

Amy Howell (12)
The Sweyne Park School

Dreams

I have a dream,
A dream of world peace,
No fighting, no war,
People who get along,
People who are kind.

A school in which homework doesn't exist,
The teachers would have more free time,
The kids would be chilled,
Less people would be in trouble.

Doctors can cure cancer
And other life-threatening illnesses,
More lives would be saved,
People wouldn't have to go through losing someone.

My last dream is that my family are healthy,
They live to an old age,
They always stay close together
And never have fight.

Ellis Davis (11)
The Sweyne Park School

Dreams!

D reams are made when I fall asleep at night
R eally scary or nice and soft, that makes me fall to sleep
E xciting dreams that keep me awake but there's one dream
A dream that the whole country lives in peace without war
or hunger

M y dream I hope will come true
S o it makes our lives better for me and you!

Hayley Waggon (13)
The Sweyne Park School

Dreams!

I have a dream,
A dream of worldwide peace,
Of justice, friendship
And no more war!

I also have a dream,
A selfish me, me dream,
That I could be famous,
A singer, an actress, a star!

And then there is this dream,
That everybody has,
That they could get
Just what they want,
But if everyone had their dream,
What would the world be like?

Lily Cook (11)
The Sweyne Park School

Dream!

I had a dream one night,
That didn't seem quite right,
About a crazy moose,
Who liked to drink a lot of juice.

He played a lot of football
And really thought he was cool,
But in fact he couldn't kick a ball at all!

All his friends would laugh
Cos he was always puffed out before the first half!
He was a crazy moose,
Who liked to drink a lot of juice!

Ben Franklin (11)
The Sweyne Park School

Dream

I have a dream . . .

That the world is at peace, that there aren't any wars,
no fighting or no amount of people being treated differently.

I have a dream . . .

That life is endless, that the world is made of sweets,
that there is actually a Heaven
and that you can talk to friends or family that have died.

I have a dream . . .

That there is a cure for cancer, that there are no bad illnesses
but if there are they can be cured.

I have a dream . . .

That all people are rich and that everyone can meet their favourite
movie star or singer.

I have a dream!
I have a dream!

Molly Humphreys (11)
The Sweyne Park School

Dream

I had a dream that there was world peace
I had a dream that I had a fast car
I had a dream that there was no poverty
I had a dream that I had an Xbox 360
I had a dream that there was no war
I had a dream that I had a plasma TV on my wall
I had a dream that there was no famine
I had a dream that there was no homework.

James Prince (13)
The Sweyne Park School

Dream

I have a dream
A dream of no animals being killed
A dream of everyone being happy
No wars, no guns and no disease
No hungry mouths to feed

I have a dream
A dream of love and peace
A dream of a world with people sharing
No bullies
But everyone caring

I have a dream
A small dream of mine
A dream the world is made of chocolate
And a small other thing; that you can pause time

I have a dream
A small dream of mine
A dream that I have a white horse
And a small other little thing,
That everyone is happy.

Claudia Shaw (11)
The Sweyne Park School

Dreams

I have a dream!
I dream of happiness and peace throughout the world.
That the world is a better place.
I dream that there will be red skies at night -
and that there will be no more war and no more fight.
I dream about rainbows and the sun -
and that everyone will be happy and all have good fun!
I dream that you can go in a shop and come out with every
                                        single shoe!
I cross my fingers that it will all come true.

Katie Rankin (11)
The Sweyne Park School

Dreams

My dream is for world peace
My dream is to be a pro golfer

My dream is to stop global warming
My dream is to be rich

My dream is to stop violence
My dream is to marry a beautiful girl

My dream is to stop child slavery
My dream is to have 2 kids, 1 boy, 1 girl

My dream is to stop poverty
My dream is to be the richest man who ever lived

My dream is to stop terrorism
My dream is to be the most known person in the world.

Ben Cox (13)
The Sweyne Park School

Rich!

I dreamt one night,
I won loads of money
And for one moment,
My whole world was sunny,
'I'm rich,' I said, as I lay asleep
And all that money I would have to peep.
There it is, lots of cash,
Let's go round the shops and spend it in a dash,
Jumpers, coats, clothing galore
And all my eyes see and more!
There were big houses and jets and friends galore,
But as money talks I wanted more.
As my dream ended and the end was in sight,
I awoke to the most horrific sight.
I was not rich, maybe one day!

Jaymee Wilkinson (11)
The Sweyne Park School

The Football Dream

Goooaaalll! What a finish by the football player of the year,

Bradley Batt.

The crowds are going wild!
He's scored his tenth goal for his new club, West Ham FC
And that in only two games!
(After the match Batt goes into the changing rooms).

'Hello Batt. Some good finishing out there.
Look, would you like to come to Barcelona FC,
Playing with some star players such as Ronaldinho,
Thierry Henry, Lionel Massi and Eto'o said Frank Rykard.
'Yes, I will come,' said Batt.

Gooaaalll! What a goal, it's Batt's sixteenth goal in five games.
He's won player of the year at Barcelona now,
Despite winning it at West Ham.

Batt goes on to be a legend and the all-time greatest player ever
And the top scorer with the most goals of 1600.

Bradley Batt (11)
The Sweyne Park School

Dreamzz . . .

As I close my eyes and drift to sleep . . .
I see a star that is my dream.
My dad so strong with a determined face
Lifting a weight weighing 115kg.
Then suddenly as I'm watching him
I hear the alphabet being sang . . .
A, B, C, D, E . . . it goes
And I laugh and laugh to find it's my bro!
I giggle to the floor and tears fall from my eyes
And then I wake up to a big surprise!
My sister counting the number line! 1, 2, 3, 4 . . .

Jaime-Leigh Mason (11)
The Sweyne Park School

I Have A Dream

I have a dream that one day
the world will be a better place.
There will be no more pollution in the air,
no cars or planes turning the skies black with filth.
I have a dream that one day
there will be no logging companies tearing down the rainforest
and killing all that is left of our forests.
I have a dream that there will be no more hunting or mindless wars
and that we will live in peace and harmony together,
because together we can make these dreams become true
so our children will have a better life.

Matt Dunt
The Sweyne Park School

Wonderful Dream

I have a dream that I play for Spurs
And world poverty never occurs.

I played centre back,
Poor people don't drink from a crack.

I can drink at thirteen in a bar,
Everyone in the world can afford a car.

I play for England and many more,
People on the street won't be poor.

Also my hair gelled on its own,
The streets are like Bugsy Malone.

I go on holiday and meet Bobby Moore
And the world never again has a war.

Dale Bliss (13)
The Sweyne Park School

Dreams

If I had a dream . . .

My dream is for world peace
My dream is to be a professional football player

My dream is to stop global warming
My dream is to be the richest man alive

My dream is to stop poverty
My dream is to have 2 kids

My dream is for no violence
My dream is to marry the world's prettiest girl

My dream is to play for Arsenal
My dream is for all the bad people to be in jail

My dream is to be famous
My dream is to get grade As in everything!

Jaydon Kinnaird (13)
The Sweyne Park School

Dreams

I dream of a world without any war,
To make people rich, no longer poor,
I dream peace in every place,
To put a smile upon every face,
I also dream every night,
Of my football team in the top flight,
For me to score the winning goal,
Against a team from the North Pole,
The final minute of extra time,
I want the cup to be mine,
An overhead kick from outside the box,
I score a goal that stops the clocks,
So that's the dream I have all the time,
I want the world to be fine.

Charlie Jones (13)
The Sweyne Park School

Dream

Every night when I go to bed,
On my pillow I lay my head.
I close my eyes and start to dream,
In colour, like the movie screen.

I dream of things I really like,
Often riding on my bike,
Or scary rides at Pleasurewood Hills,
That go so fast they give me chills.

Of all my friends and my new school,
Although it's big it's really cool,
I dream of things I like to eat,
The ones my mum says are a treat.

I can't wait to go to bed,
For dreams to pop into my head,
They are fun as you can see
And different every night for me.

Kathryn Bowen (11)
The Sweyne Park School

Dream

I have a dream, a dream of living forever,
wouldn't it be great, but also . . .

Rivers of chocolate would be nice,
gushing downstream.

Living forever, doing everything you wanted
and needed forever, however.

Wouldn't it be great if everyone was rich
and money grew on trees.

That's my dream tonight and forever.

Ellie Berry (12)
The Sweyne Park School

Dream

I toss and turn,
During the night,
Looking at things,
And searching for light.

As I fall
Into a very deep sleep,
I dream a dream
I wish I could keep.

In my dream,
I walk about,
In a very strange place,
Without a doubt.

I find a room,
So colourful and bright,
Full of lots of things,
That bring me delight.

I sit in this room,
For hours and hours,
Listening and playing,
With everything in my power.

Then as I listen,
I hear a ringing bell,
I jolted awake
And away the dream fell.

Rachel Steddon (13)
The Sweyne Park School

Dreams

I dreamt that I was a dancer,
Dancing all day and night.
I dreamt that I was a dancer,
Under the spotlight.

I dreamt I was a princess,
With a golden crown.
I dreamt I was a princess,
The coolest one in town.

I dreamt I was a fairy,
Flying in the sky.
I dreamt I was a fairy,
Way up high.

I dreamt I was a pop star,
Because I'm at that age.
I dreamt I was a pop star,
Singing loud on stage.

I dreamt I was a model,
Down the catwalk I go.
I dreamt I was a model,
About fashion I must know.

Those dreams from when I was younger,
I used to say would come true,
But now they seem so far away,
Because, I know as an adult, there is work to do!

Hollie Robinson (12)
The Sweyne Park School

Yume - Dream - Tanka

Beauty of surreal
That is always known to us
Teach me to believe
In waking you long to dream
In dreaming you long to wake.

Lucy Hollington (16)
The Sweyne Park School

Dream Poem

I lay on my head,
on my bed,
where I sleep and dream and snore.

When I go to a place,
with lots of space,
just outside my door.

I go back in time,
where magic is fine,
and fly up into the sky.

I fight in war,
with the Romans, corr,
believe me I don't lie.

I kill Achilles,
and Archimedes,
with fire flying from my eyes.

Then I wake up,
do normal stuff
and eat a nice pork pie.

Sam Paterson (11)
The Sweyne Park School

Dream

I have a dream
A dream of me
Being a scientist
That's my dream.
I'd bring peace and justice
All over the world
Taking starvation away
In my red Ferrari
I'd rule the world
Just me and my friends.

Joshua Edwards (11)
The Sweyne Park School

Dreams

In my dreams . . .

I dreamt that world poverty was ended
and I could help all the starving children,
that all terrorists were gone, we didn't have any . . . at all.
Everybody was friends with everybody
and we had world peace.
Mostly everybody walked everywhere
and we didn't have much pollution at all,
the ozone layer was closing up,
everything was recycled!
There were lots of singers but their CDs
were made from environmentally friendly material
and mostly everything was made
from environmentally friendly materials.

I dreamt that I was an aeroplane soaring through the blue sky,
I dreamt that I was an aeroplane and it made me wonder why!
How did I become this? Would I be able to kiss?
But the answer was no . . . I could never love again,
I was just a piece of scrap metal
that flew people to their destinations . . .
that's all I would be,
an aeroplane . . . an aeroplane.

Chloe Humphreys (13)
The Sweyne Park School

Dreams

D aydreams, delightful dreams
R iveting dreams
E ntertaining, exciting
A mazing dreams
M ysterious, marvellous
S cary or sad.

Matthew Smith (13)
The Sweyne Park School

Dreams

I dream that the world was made of chocolate
And the trees were made of gold.
I wish that school was only part time
And Ashton scored the winning goal.

If everyone took a little time to care for one another,
There may not be so many wars
And hunger is kept at bay from so many doors.

I wish that homework could be banned,
So I have more time to play around.
I could spend my time on the computer,
Walk the dogs for my mum, that would really suit her.

Marissa Parmenter (13)
The Sweyne Park School

Dreams

I have a dream,
a dream of world peace,
no more wars.

I have a dream
people have a future
and a happy life.

> I have a dream
> that there is no more
> homework or school
>
> I have a dream
> about chocolate bars
> falling from the sky.

If only they were true.

Hannah Thomas (13)
The Sweyne Park School

My Dream

I am the first person on Mars,
Next I am laying on a hammock in Hawaii,
Then I'm performing on the last night of the proms,
Next I am playing Joseph in Joseph and the
Technicolour Dreamcoat in the West End,
Then I am walking around the pyramids of Gaza,
Next I am exploring a dense rainforest,
Then I am playing for England in goal,
Oh, I have just conceded a goal,
The manager gets out a gun and fires,
Then I land back in bed,
'Oh,' I said to myself, 'that must have been a dream!'

Peter Lang (11)
The Sweyne Park School

Dreams

I have a dream,
a dream of life,
a dream of world peace.
But also I have a dream about chocolate
becoming the most healthiest thing in the world.

World peace would be great,
no wars, fighting and everyone would get along.
Healthy chocolate, I could eat it all day and not get fat.

Healthy chocolate, world peace,
Why can't they both just come true?

Erin Moorby (11)
The Sweyne Park School

Dreamy Dream

Dreams, dreams over there,
Can it be true or is it some chair?
I wonder if it is really true,
All I just want is to meet you.

I saw you running over the hill,
Or was it someone trying to kill?
I have this gift I like for you,
I just hope that you like it too.

But then one day we came face to face
And my heart was beating like a race.
I was speechless and didn't know what to say,
So sadly I just ran away.

To this day I still remember what happened then,
To think, it was years ago, nearly about ten.
But right now I regret what I had done,
I really just wish I hadn't have run.

All of a sudden I heard a really loud *bang!*
But then I looked, my alarm had rang.
It was 7am, time for school,
The whole thing was a dream! Nothing really cool.

Thamanna Khan (13)
The Sweyne Park School

Dreams

Dreams are creations of the mind,
Whence awake and asleep.
Revives lost loved ones,
Evokes forgotten emotions.

Chasing personal pursuits,
Leading different lives,
But with dreams,
Come nightmares.

Alex Brown (13)
The Sweyne Park School

Sleep Poem . . .

Sleep, sleep, fall asleep
And dream of brighter times . . .

Jump, skip, dance around
And think of songs that rhyme . . .

Scream, yell, cry and shout
For such a dream to end . . .

Jumping, skipping, crying out
Just drives me round the bend.

Chocolate bunnies, flying pigs
Sweet buttercups and chewy figs . . .

Nightmare, horror, cruel and pain
Girly girls, very vain . . .

Silver, shining, moonlit sky
Asking, thinking, wondering
Why . . .

Megan Gargate (13)
The Sweyne Park School

My Dream

I had a dream,
I dreamt of a quad,
I had a dream,
I dreamt of Princess the dog,
I had a dream,
I dreamt of chocolate,
My dreams may come true
Or maybe not,
I have to find out
As I sleep tonight.

Dannii-Ella Ingram (11)
The Sweyne Park School

Dreams

Dreams of magic princesses and glitter,
Not horror dreams that make you shiver!
Falling off the kerbs, makes you go jump,
Then you wake up with those things called goosebumps,
A chilly feeling down your spine, going down in a line.
Dreams of what you want to be when you are older,
Hmmm . . . maybe a person who works with soldier!
My dream is to become a beautician,
Or maybe even a nail technician.
Whatever the dream may be
Do not leave for others to see . . .
Because they may take it away!

Lauren Jones (12)
The Sweyne Park School

Dreams

Dreams, dreams, so very strange,
Sometimes complete gobbledegook,
We can enjoy them and hate them,
You could be in the RAF,
Or falling off a cliff.

Dreams, dreams, so very fun,
You could see your dead grandad,
Or do something you always wanted to do,
Then something bad happens and it becomes
A nightmare!

This is when you are scared,
It all goes wrong,
A dinosaur could be chasing you,
Or . . . or . . . or . . . taking a maths test
Argh!

Jack Woolley (12)
The Sweyne Park School

Dreams

At night I dream about winning a fortune,
I wake up and I feel disappointed.
At night I dream about being famous,
I wake up and I feel disappointed.
At night I dream about having a designer wardrobe,
I wake up and I feel disappointed.

At day I daydream about being out shopping with my friends,
I come back to real life and I'm sitting in class.
At day, I daydream about being at an Arsenal game,
I come back to real life and I'm shopping with my parents.
Maybe someday I won't feel disappointed.

Rebecca Chatfield (13)
The Sweyne Park School

My Dream

My dream is to become a rally driver,
Skidding around corners,
Then putting my foot right down on the accelerator.
'Sharp left,' says the navigator,
I go into the corner perfectly,
My back end swings round,
I can hardly see out of my window,
I accelerate and cross the line.

I look at the time,
First place is mine.

Ethan Hawkins (12)
The Sweyne Park School

My Dream, My Future

Do you want to know my dream
Or do you want to know my future, I wonder?
I will try to link them together as they both have similarities.

I start my dream alone,
On an empty West End stage.
Then suddenly, lights, noise, action.
Everyone's singing, acting and dancing.

My heart is pounding as I hear my cue,
Out of the wings I run,
At centre stage I stop.
I lift my eyes and sing.

My last note I hold and it seems an eternity.
The note fades out and the applause fills my heart with joy,
Everyone stands upon their feet.

We take our bow and return their smiles,
You see, everyone can fulfil their dream.

Everyone, including you.

Lucy Judd (12)
The Sweyne Park School

Dream

A dream can be a nightmare when you are lost and scared,
But sometimes in this nightmare there's good and you are spared.
It's this random choosing that makes a dream a dream,
It's all actually nothing, although scary it may seem.
To dream you don't have to be on your back or even fast asleep,
You can have them all through the day, hence the name 'daydream'.
For dreams are mysterious and a secret only I know,
I'll let you in on this, but you'll have to wait until tomorrow.

Connor Jennings (11)
The Sweyne Park School

A Dream

A dream is something random,
A thing that's really odd,
It could be about chickens,
About chocolate, cats and dogs.

A dream is always different,
Or maybe it's the same,
Dreams that stem from memories,
Muddled in your brain.

A dream can be a nightmare,
To others it may be,
Some lovely dream they wished for,
Or a crazy mystery.

Harriet Bass-Tidman (13)
The Sweyne Park School

Dreams

As you lie in your bed at night,
You wonder what adventure you'll go on tonight,
You could go back in time,
Work in a mine
And even go to space!

As you drift off to sleep,
You take a great leap
And find yourself in a dream!

As you take a look around,
There is nothing to be found,
Then you realise you're not in a dream at all
And you body is taken to hospital!

Joe Woodward (13)
The Sweyne Park School

My Dream

I'm lying asleep in bed . . . dreaming . . .
Dreaming that I can speak to things that aren't human,
Dreaming about a place where gods go to war.

I'm dreaming about a boat that takes warriors away to
$\qquad$ protect the king,

Dreaming that I can use traps to catch birds,
Dreaming that I'm in a shop where I can buy strong armour.

Dreaming a dream called Runescape.

Henry Wood (12)
The Sweyne Park School

Dreams!

Dreams can make everything seem possible
I could fly!
Dreams can make reality disappear
I could climb the highest mountain
Dreams can make you feel invincible
I can run faster than an Olympic runner!
Dreams can be scary or happy
I can jump on clouds!
Dreams are your time to let your
Imagination run wild!

Danielle Knight (13)
The Sweyne Park School

A Dream

D reams are meant to be . . .
R elaxing and . . .
E very night your dreams should be . . .
A mazing and . . .
M agical at the same time . . .

Amy Nisbett (13)
The Sweyne Park School

Dreams

D reams can be good and they can be bad, they feel so
R eal but they are not. Anything can happen
E ven the most unimaginable things.
A ll of them are different, they can
M ake you happy or sad and all of this happens while you
S leep!

          Z
        Z
          Z
            Z.

Alex Hawkins (14)
The Sweyne Park School

Dreams

When I fall asleep I dream of happy things,
When I fall asleep I dream of unhappy things.
When I dream I dream of angels,
When I dream I dream of devils,
When I dream I dream of monkeys,
When I dream I dream of gorillas.
When I fall asleep I dream of good and bad things,
When I dream,
When I dream . . .

Jack Keys (13)
The Sweyne Park School

My Dream

Before I went to bed the night before,
I took a thought about my dog that passed away not long ago,
As I got into bed I remembered back to when we used to play,
As I drifted off to sleep I remembered those days,
I dreamt about that night, that he was with me again,
To play with again.

Adam Bridges (13)
The Sweyne Park School

What Is A Dream?

A dream.
What is a dream?
How does it happen?
A dream, a dream.

You could be far away
Or at home,
Anywhere in the world.
A dream, a dream.

You could be your favourite action hero,
Sports star, role model,
Anyone you want.
A dream, a dream.

It's a weird thing.
Is it the future
Or is it just your imagination playing games?
A dream, a dream.

You could be playing football,
Doing your dream job, reading a book,
Anything you want to be or do.
A dream, a dream.

You could be playing with friends,
Talking, arguing.
Anything that you want to happen.
A dream, a dream.

A dream.
What is a dream?
How does is happen?
A dream, a dream . . .

Esther Lang (14)
The Sweyne Park School

Dreaming

A dream is like
A wish come true
I may have had it before
It may well be new

It's so surreal
To have a dream
In one of them
My name was Mr Bean

Sometimes you even
Have a nightmare
They can be so frightening
Spikes are formed all over my hair

There can always be
Déjà vu
Sometimes you see friends
Sometimes you see you.

Jordan Roberts (13)
The Sweyne Park School

I Have A Dream

A dream of wisdom and ability to do
Things I never thought I could do.
But I still want a big mansion.

I would love to have peace in the world
And a brand new Ferrari.

No wars, no fighting,
But a massive, healthy chocolate cake for me.

No disasters in the world,
But I could still have lots of money.

No starvation and no world hunger,
Just save lots of nice stuff for me.

Dean Bonning (12)
The Sweyne Park School

Nightmare In Bed

He shot down the man obstructing him from the safe,
before picking up his axe
and smashing down the solid steel door.

He ran to his getaway car,
with over £1 million,
only to find that the police were trailing him.

He got his accomplice to drive,
whilst the man shot,
however he crashed.

He screamed,
only to awake, sweating like mad.
Thank god. It was only a dream.

Kym Marsh (12)
The Sweyne Park School

Dragon Dream

I fought a dragon day and night
The dragon once had a terrible fright
Of me becoming a brave knight!
One of us saw the light
Which one you say?
Let's save it for another day
This is in my dream to stay
No one can take that away!
Dragons are like me and you
They have hearts, brains and feelings too!
Treat them with respect
And then you'll get respect too!

Lacey Beels (12)
The Sweyne Park School

Dreams

Dreams are strange
Dreams are weird
When have you heard of a girl with a beard
Or ice cream made in ovens?

You can dream things that happen tomorrow
Some involve sorrow
They can be very happy
Or even be about a dog in a nappy!

Sam Vincent (13)
The Sweyne Park School

What If . . .

What if a dream is about a fairy tale.
What if a dream is about your family.
What if a dream is about your friends.
What if a dream is about your nightmare.
What if a dream is about someone you love,
Or close to you.
Dreams can be all shapes and sizes.

Kayleigh Roffey (13)
The Sweyne Park School

Dreams!

I was lying in my bed when I fell asleep,
I was in a deep sleep.
I could run, I could fly,
I could jump to touch the sky.
Sheep bounced past on fluffy clouds,
Was I shouting really loud?
Could anybody hear *me?*

Emily Little (13)
The Sweyne Park School

Departing

I am departing, I'm going to die
I'm going to Heaven where peaceful souls lie

This isn't good, this isn't bad
Though this world makes people sad

I never felt pain in my life
Though it was filled with trouble and strife

Death is a start, life is the end
That always was the common trend

Here I am being judged by God
He could end my life with a simple nod

The gates swing open, in I walk
Supported by clouds white as chalk

No darkness, no flame, no Devil at all
Just a bright light, that is all.

Lewis Smith (12)
The Sweyne Park School

Dreams

Night flurries,
Days pass,
None seem to matter,
I'm asleep without worries,

Dream to nightmare,
The night wastes away,
I fight back the darkness,
I win with valour, now I'm back there,

In my land of dreams,
It's day again,
I awake,
But life is not what it seems.

Jack Spicer (14)
The Sweyne Park School

Dreams

Dreams are good,
Dreams are bad,
Some are nasty,
Some are fun.

Sometimes you feel scared,
Sometimes you feel happy,
Either way,
Soon it will end.

You could be invincible,
You could be invisible,
You could be wealthy,
You could be poor.

You will wake up,
Forget what you dreamt,
Only remembering details,
Of last night's events!

Connor Addington (13)
The Sweyne Park School

Dreamzzz

A dream is a happy thing
Doing what you do best
Or doing what you would like to do
Maybe beating all the rest

Flying out to outerspace
Or running in your favourite race
At the end a flash of light
You've been dreaming all night.

Lewis Jones (13)
The Sweyne Park School

Dream

When you lay awake at night, do you wish you could be dreaming?
Of magical lands and pirate ships so colourful it's beaming,
Then you fall asleep,
You're in your dream world, but which dream should you take?
You find your lucky number but is that the right one for you?
Oh what shall we do?
Then you go through the door wondering what it might be,
But then you see your dreamland in front of you,
Then your mind goes wild and wanders with you too,
But then you fall down a ditch, oh what shall you do?
But you can't get out, seems like you are going to be stuck
                                                        there forever,
Then your mind thinks, *oh I shall be clever*
And wakes you up in the middle of the night
And gives you a big fright,
But you go to sleep again,
Then in the morning you wake up and say I am a superstar again,
You thought you wouldn't tell anyone and keep it to yourself,
Because people might laugh,
But your wishes might come true,
So keep on holding on to them, your wishes might come true
Then one day your ultimate wish might come true too.

Natalie Pavelin (11)
The Sweyne Park School

Dream Poem

D reams can be about anything you want
    and can either be good or bad,
R eading before bed can lead to a dream, happy or sad,
E very dream is possible, I'm sure you're glad,
A bout what you want when you want it to be
M agical things happen, can't you see!

Michaela Piper (11)
The Sweyne Park School

Dreams

As I close my eyes and begin to fall asleep
I start to dream of wonderful things
And people I'd like to meet.
My mind whizzes with imagination
Of things I'd like to do like . . .
Being a fish or granting a wish
Or being in a fairy tale or two!

Summer White (11)
The Sweyne Park School

My Poem

F ootball is a game of two halves.
O ne team of eleven versus the other.
O ne captain of each team.
T wo goals.
B alls flying everywhere.
A ll of the team must be working hard.
L ots of
L uscious green pitches to play on.

Dexter Brunt (11)
The Sweyne Park School

Dreams

One night I had a dream
That I visited a faraway place
And I ate some cream
I got it all over the place
But it was all just a dream so
I ran all over the place.

James Proctor (11)
The Sweyne Park School

My Dream

M y random dreams with no screams,
Y ou're not going to believe it.

D reaming all night of me as the creator
R unning miles and miles across desert land
E ntering the fine lord's temple.
A ggravating and killing all in my way.
M eet a fine princess called Aura
S et out to find the ever-living humans
      and the portal to the world of the everlasting war.

Michael Heather (11)
The Sweyne Park School

Flying

I'm laying in bed, asleep.
Dreaming.
Dreaming of travelling the world.
In a hot air balloon.
Only a basket under my feet.
Dreaming of landing.

In another country, trying the foods and having fun.
Then take off again.

I feel the hot air above.
I'm flying!
I look down and see the ocean.
The land.
An island in the middle of the sea.
All by myself.
I've discovered an island.
I want to name it, tell the world.
So I move again.
Without the balloon, I'm flying.
But it's only a dream.

Jarrad Saul (11)
The Sweyne Park School

My Dream

First of all I went to bed, I got in
and burrowed my head.

I dreamt of big battles and stormy seas,
I dreamt of candle wax and lots of bees.
There I was with the Queen shaking her hand
and flying an aeroplane, getting ready to land.

But your life may not be how it seems,
after all, life is nothing but
                              Dreams.

Jake Szabo (11)
The Sweyne Park School

First Impressions

Sweyne Park School is great,
I never want to be late.
I just about know who my teachers are,
I've been reciting their names in the car!

If I have any worries,
I'll go to pupil services in a hurry.
The ladies are always there to help you,
Whether you're sick or your money's due!

The lessons are fun,
Like a Belgian bun!
The home learning is not too hard,
But I'd rather be playing down the park.

Although I've only been here a short time,
The friends that I've made have been kind.
So here is to five more years of school,
Let's hope I don't become a fool!

George Barker (11)
The Sweyne Park School

Dreams

D reams are random, black, white and multicoloured
   and all shapes and sizes.
R eally wild dreams have different planets
   or are life-changing experiences.
E xperiences you have had, holidays, scares
   or happy memories, all in your dreams.
A dream could be something that you have done
   that haunts you for the rest of your life.
M emories are powerful if they're real or not,
   or it may be something scary.
S cary or not they're in your head, I once dreamt that
   I was my brother and I was hit by a car.

Ryan Beckwith (11)
The Sweyne Park School

My Dream

When you have a scary dream
And you have had a bad scare
And all you want to do is scream,
Just you hang in there.
You try to tell your mum it's true,
But all she does is giggle,
She obviously doesn't believe you,
She makes your squirm and wriggle,
You picture the things on the wall,
To be the monsters you have seen,
They range from big to small,
By the time you get to sleep all the night has been.

Melissa Traynor (11)
The Sweyne Park School

Young Writers Information

We hope you have enjoyed reading this book - and that you will continue to enjoy it in the coming years.

If you like reading and writing poetry drop us a line, or give us a call, and we'll send you a free information pack.

Alternatively if you would like to order further copies of this book or any of our other titles, then please give us a call or log onto our website at www.youngwriters.co.uk

Young Writers Information
Remus House
Coltsfoot Drive
Peterborough
PE2 9JX

(01733) 890066